H.M.S. "BEDOU

and

THE LONG MARCH

To those with whom I sailed and served in peace and war, especially to those of H.M.S. "BEDOUIN", whose memory stays with me always.

H.M.S. "BEDOUIN" *and* THE LONG MARCH HOME

PERCY HAGGER

NAVIGATOR BOOKS

Published by Navigator Books
Ringwood, Hampshire

ISBN 0 902830 28 7

Typeset by Moorhouse Typesetters
Printed by The Cromwell Press, Melksham, Wiltshire

CHAPTER ONE

Joining up, and joining H.M.S. "BEDOUIN"

According to the Drafting Office at Chatham, H.M.S. "BEDOUIN" was lying at Wallsend-on-Tyne having completed a refit. I had to catch a train from Chatham to Charing Cross in the early evening. At Charing Cross there would be Naval lorries to transport any ratings to whatever other station they had to go to. I had to go to Kings Cross and catch the 22.00 to Newcastle-on-Tyne, and there report to the R.T.O.

It was a Saturday that I went on draft, and it would be early Sunday morning when the train arrived at Newcastle. Although I had all my belongings to cart around with me, I had with me a Signalman from "BEDOUIN" who had, for some reason, had his leave extended, and was now travelling with me to rejoin "BEDOUIN". His very presence was a boon, and he also helped me to trot my kit from place to place.

The train arrived at Newcastle about 05.00. How deserted a main line railway station can be at that hour in the morning, even a very busy one normally. Eventually, finding one of the station staff, he informed us that the R.T.O. would not open for business until 08.00; apparently Sunday opening time. What to do for almost three hours? Well, the fellow did say that I could leave my gear in a safe place, and he did mention that a certain cafe might just be open at that unearthly hour. No such luck, though, and it left the two of us with the prospect of having to wait almost an hour and a half before, according to his menu of opening and closing times, the cafe would be available for refreshment of a kind. The only thing to do became clear, walk, or catch a severe cold waiting in the draughty station. We walked. At 07.00 we ambled back to the cafe and managed to procure a cup of tea each.

Just before 08.00 we arrived outside the R.T.O. When they arrived, about ten minutes later, and after they had shuffled through a pile of draft orders and ship movements, we were kindly informed that "BEDOUIN" had sailed at 07.00 and that we would have to go to Scapa to join her.

Being very kind at heart, the gentlemen of the R.T.O. provided us with meal vouchers for the day, and gave us travel warrant, time-table, and a further stock of meal vouchers. We had to catch a train at 00.20 Monday morning for Carlisle, where we would have to change and catch another to Perth, the whole day would be ours to do as we wished. I can assure you that, even in wartime, there was very little going on in Newcastle on a Sunday, and very few places to get anything to eat.

Shortly afterwards the pair of us found where the train was hiding and got my kit aboard, then found an empty compartment and settled down to get some sleep. The train we were due to catch at Carlisle arrived there at about 02.55. That meant that we would have about twenty minutes to wait, should the train we were on now arrive on time, (usually unlikely in wartime), but as this one was an early morning train, strangely enough it did get in on time.

The train from Carlisle was a sleeper from Euston to Perth, therefore there were only a limited number of ordinary coaches on it. Having loaded my kit aboard, the pair of is were faced with the problem of finding a seat. Despite the large number of Servicemen travelling, we found a couple of seats in the same compartment with comparative ease. This train was due at Perth at 07.00.

All ex-Servicemen will recall rail travel in those days, struggling along corridors piled with kitbags and cases, not to mention sleeping bodies; sliding back compartment doors in the search for a seat, curtains drawn, the clackety-clack of the darkened train seeming to go on for ever. Everybody in uniform, mostly sleeping or trying to, all with their private thoughts and fears.

My own thoughts went back to H.M.S. "GANGES" which I had joined as a Boy Seaman in 1937, moving after preliminary training to H.M.S. "RAMILLIES", a 29,000 ton battleship with eight 15 inch guns. How easily I had slipped into Navy ways and routines, the terms and traditions that were shaping my life with stirring moments, too, like being part of the shipboard ceremony with bugles playing at Sunset and The Last Post.

I was part of it, too, when "RAMILLIES" took part in the Fleet Review of 1938 and we were there with "NELSON", (Flagship), "RODNEY", "ROYAL SOVEREIGN", "ROYAL OAK", "REVENGE", "HOOD", "RENOWN", "ARK ROYAL", "COURAGEOUS", "FURIOUS", "HERMES" plus cruisers and twenty-seven destroyers.

Looking around at my sleeping companions in the clattering train, most of them older than me yet new to their uniforms, I realised how lucky I was to have had this service experience to prepare me for what was to come.

And thinking back to all the activity there was about the time of the 1938 Fleet Review, activity to bring the fleet to a state of readiness; "RAMILLIES" went straight from the Review to Devonport Dockyard and I was moved to "RESOLUTION". The September crisis had changed her from Boy's Training Ship to a member ship of the Fleet. Then, who could fail to remember Neville Chamberlain flying back from Germany, waving his piece of paper and telling us that it would be peace in our time. By Christmas 1938 we were even told that Hitler was no more than a music hall joke. And so after the crisis was over, (so everybody thought), "RESOLUTION" carried on fully commissioned with a normal peacetime crew. An important naval appointment was made in that ship in May 1939 when I was rated Able Seaman. I was 18½ years old.

Three months later "ROYAL SOVEREIGN" surrendered the flag to "RESOLUTION" and we were Flagship, Rear Admiral Western Approaches.

In September Mr. Chamberlain spoke to us again on the radio and we then knew we were at war. Not long afterwards I was told to report to the Drafting Office at Chatham and my days in the big ships came to an end. I was sent to do my Seaman Torpedoman's course at H.M.S. "VERNON", and then back to Chatham to await whatever the Drafting Office had in store for me.

All these thoughts and memories came flooding back to me, mixed in with uneasy sleep until our arrival at Perth, where we had to change once more. The next train took us to Inverness, where it arrived just before 10.00. Change trains again, and the train for Thurso left at 11.00, but mind you were in the right half, because it split at the last station before Thurso, and the rear half went on to Wick.

The hour wait gave us plenty of time to replenish our food supplies, for we were getting very good service from the kindly canteen ladies at the end of the station platform at Inverness, they piled us up for the value of one of our meal vouchers.

Travelling through the highlands of Scotland is a wonderful sight. One could be forgiven for forgetting that we were at war, everything seemed to be so tranquil in that mountainous area. Names on some of the stations that still sported them were familiar, Dingwall, Invergordon, Cromarty and such places. However, all good things come to an end sometimes, and darkness closed in, blotting out the scenery, and blinds had to be drawn on the train windows. About 18.00 we arrived at Thurso, where transport awaited us, and we were taken to a hall, where we could get a meal and a bed for the night, for we had to be up early the next morning to be taken to the harbour and on to the Scapa ferry, the steamship St. Ninian.

The St. Ninian was the only ferry to be operating between the mainland and the Orkneys. Her first stop after passing through the boom was at Lyness, where most of the destroyers berthed after refuelling on arrival. There also lay the local floating transit hotel, H.M.S. (late S.S.) "DUNLUCE CASTLE", a vessel of the Union Castle Line, which had been rescued from the scrap yard at the outbreak of war. She apparently had staggered some of the way to Scapa under her own power, but had broken down and was unrepairable, and had finished the journey being ignominiously towed to her berth at Lyness. One could also see the shape of another old warrior, H.M.S. "IRON DUKE". She had been the Boys's Sea Training Ship at Portsmouth before war broke out, and in 1916 had been the Flagship of Admiral Jellicoe at the Battle of Jutland, and also serving aboard, as a Lieutenant was our present King, George VI.

There also further down from Lyness lay the upturned hull of the German Navy battleship of 1919 which had been scuttled there in Scapa Flow. It was the very last one to be raised, and was destined to stay at Scapa for the deration of the war. Her name "DERFFLINGER" and brought back memories for me of my father who had served on H.M.S. "PHAETON", the light cruiser that escorted the German High Seas Fleet into Scapa Flow where they were promptly scuttled.

After a couple of days aboard "DUNLUCE CASTLE", the pair of us were sitting down having a natter on the top hold deck which is just below the upper deck. Going to the rails, one could see right down into the hold. On each of the decks below the upper deck there were various store rooms. This particular evening, after a while, we both looked at each other and voiced the same question, "Do you smell smoke?". Yes, we did smell smoke, and on looking around us, first on the deck we were on, and then peering down into the hold spaces below and at the deck below, at last we espied smoke creeping out from one of the storeroom doors.

Prompt action was required, so off went 'Bunts' to raise the alarm, while I stayed on the spot to watch for any complications, and to point out the offending storeroom. The panic that announcement caused would have gone down well in a Laurel and Hardy film. There were frantic efforts to get the ship ready for slipping the buoy and possibly going aground, so as not to be a menace to the warships moored there.

It became evident that the mooring shackle would never be undone by ordinary methods, which meant being unable to slip the buoy, so other ways and means were being tried, such as hacksaws. However, on the arrival of the fire party at the scene of the crime, and with the arrival simultaneously of the 'Jack Dusty', as Stores Branch members were known as, complete with key, the seat of the fire soon became apparent, and with a little wetting down of the smouldering blankets stowed in that storeroom, and the quick removal of them from the store, the fire was quickly quenched, and peace reigned once more.

A day or two later "BEDOUIN" appeared and we two were able to board our own ship. A quick joining routine done, I went down into what was to be my home, dining room, bedroom and recreation room all rolled into one. After introduction to the Leading Hand of the mess, L/S Tom Kilbey, L.T.O., I had to see the T.I. P.O. Bowles, and the Torpedo Office, Mr. Tombs, Warrant Officer (non commissioned). He was the Gunner(T).

My action station for the time being would be as one of the fuse-setters on 'A' mounting during A.A. action, and as a supply number in surface action. On the work front, I would be under Tom Kilbey, low power section.

The stay in Scapa lasted until next morning, when "BEDOUIN" sailed on convoy protection duty. That trip gave me my first taste of an attack by enemy aircraft. The weather, as usual, blew a full gale, making gunnery awkward.

This trip was also my first taste of 'Canteen messing', where each mess made up it's own meals, all chef had to do was cook the food. Thus, one stormy evening, I went down to supper and there laid out for me to see and gaze at were the plates of liver and bacon. I turned back and ran for the upper deck and promptly heaved up. After that one upheaval I was right as rain, my one bout of seasickness cured.

"BEDOUIN" returned to Rosyth at the end of that trip and I found that my mother had been taken ill, and was now in an isolation

German destroyer adrift and blazing at second battle of Narvik, the victim of "BEDOUIN", "PUNJABI" and Co.

H.M.S. "COSSACK" on fire at Narvik. The fire was quickly put out.

ward of a hospital in Dartford. The Gunner(T) took me to the 1st Lt., said I could be spared, and was packed off on a 48 hour leave. On arriving home, I soon found out which hospital, leapt aboard my trusty bike and belted off to the hospital. Announcing who I was, the staff immediately dressed me up in hospital anti-germ gear, and I went in to see Ma. Whether she heard me nattering away to her I know not, but she did seem a little better when Dad and I saw her that evening.

Next morning I left for Rosyth and on arriving there, found "BEDOUIN" had sailed. Reporting to the transit ship there, H.M.S. "COCKRANE", I was sent to Scapa, put on a destroyer which took me to somewhere off Norway, and I was deposited back aboard "BEDOUIN".

German destroyer on fire and sinking,
a victim of torpedoes from H.M.S. "KIMBERLEY".

The stories of the two Naval engagements of 10th and 13th April 1940 at Narvik have been well narrated by many authors and historians. When one is in that position where not much can be seen, what can one say? I have a series of photographs at home which were taken during the action and from the Swordfish aircraft that played such an important part by pinpointing targets before we got too close and we were able to spring the surprise, not the Hun.

"COSSACK" went in too close to the shore batteries and paid the price in damage and casualties. "BEDOUIN" seemed to bear a charmed life among all the confusion around her. German torpedoes fired at us either failed to explode or blew up prematurely, but as was found out later, the German torpedo being used just did not like cold water and during both battles, the snow still lay thick on the ground, making the waters in the fiords icy cold.

I know we left one German destroyer ablaze and sinking after catching him napping, we knew where he was and were able to get in the all important first blows. With "WARSPITE" heaving a few very heavy bricks about the place, the advantage was ours. Two, who had hoped to escape went inland, up Rombaks Fiord and then ran themselves aground and the crafty pair sited their torpedo tubes on the sharp right-angled turn at the point where we would have to emerge and waited. "ESKIMO" was the unfortunate one. She copped two fish and lost her bows right up to the forward superstructure. She was lucky not to have been sunk, but was towed out to Haarstad I believe and then had a wooden dummy bow fitted, went home to U.K. and had a new bow fitted.

"BEDOUIN" received very minor damage, some shrapnel wounds in some voice pipes, and a split in the left barrel of 'A' mounting, caused no doubt by a 5.1" German shell bouncing off it. Our casualty list only had one customer, and he was not seriously hurt, a few bits of shrapnel piercing the cork life jacket he was wearing and hitting him in the back. He was soon despatched to the hospital at Haarstad and then sent home.

Now came the really nasty bit. "BEDOUIN" had to stay in the Narvik area and try to play merry hell with the German ground forces. We were desperately short of ammunition for the 4.7" guns and that meant using such as we had sparingly. one of the first targets was the power station in Rombaks Fiord, that was put out of action in a combined action with another ship.

A cruiser had arrived to assist in the destruction of the enemy on the ground, if that could be done, but first there was the railway bridge well up Rombaks Fiord. We knew this was in use by the enemy so up the fiord we went to try and knock it down. Well, yes, we did bust it up somewhat and it took jerry a long time to put it right again, only to have it bent again. In the meantime another target presented itself, a troop and supply train.

With the cruiser to help, this train was forced to take cover in a tunnel that was close to the shore and as it entered the tunnel, helped along by some encouragement given by "BEDOUIN's" 4.7" guns, it

H.M.S. "BEDOUIN" leading H.M.S. "ICARUS", fitted out for minesweeping, and H.M.S. "WARSPITE".

disappeared from sight, only to be discouraged from leaving the tunnel by a salvo of 6" shells landing in the mouth of the tunnel in front of it. Thus a game of cat and mouse ended by both "BEDOUIN" and the cruiser lobbing in shells at each end of the tunnel simultaneously. So much for the train.

German troops were gradually spreading out on the ground, but were keeping low for the time being. We though, had found a source of information. A couple of Norwegians had come out to the ship and volunteered some intelligence and we, not being sure at first, took the pair along with us, so that if this did turn out to be an ambush, the Norwegians would also suffer. They were willing and from then on, whenever they could, they brought us information which was very helpful to us.

A newly arrived destroyer, one of the old 1918 'V' and 'W' class had come to join forces with "BEDOUIN". Entering Rombaks Fiord, she went close to the shore on the Narvik side of the fiord and almost at once came under fire from an anti-tank gun which had been brought down to the foreshore unseen by us in spite of our vigilance. Receiving a hit in a boiler room, the old destroyer hastily beat a retreat, calling up the heavy mob to deal with the gun. Maybe that anti-tank weapon would have remained unnoticed for some time had it not blown its cover on that old destroyer. In went "BEDOUIN" and, closing to point blank range, fired and that was the last we heard of that German gun and crew.

Each time we heard that the bridge had been repaired and went up to upset the hard work of the Hun engineers, so we came under machine gun fire. Not that any damage was done to the ship, or any casualties caused, it was a bit like a dog having an annoying flea.

Then it came. That which we had been free of so far descended upon us, an air attack. The fiords may be deep, but in many places very narrow. Rombaks was one of these fiords which were long and narrow most of its length. The entrance from Narvik Fiord is narrow, very narrow, but opens out quickly and remains fairly wide as far as the power station where it narrows with the sharp right-hand turn immediately through the narrowed part. In such a fiord even a destroyer had to turn within its own length.

Second battle of Narvik. Tribal class destroyers in action showing H.M.S. "PUNJABI" in foreground.

With high mountains either side, one would have thought that an attack from the air might be impossible, or at least highly improbable, but these mountain top hopping German bombers had other thoughts.

The first attack came just after "BEDOUIN" had entered Rombaks Fiord and was in the middle of doing a 180° turn to port, thus bringing the ship bows to the entrance. From nowhere came the bomber and although we had some sort of warning and were closed up at action stations, there was no way we could get a shot at it. With the rudder hard aport, port engine half astern and starboard engine half ahead, we were spinning on our own axis.

We felt the ship shudder. The Captain had brought the rudder amidships and put the port engine full ahead, thus stopping the turning motion of the ship. It was this manoeuvre that must have saved us. Somebody suddenly shouted out "The bastard's dropped his shit". The next moment a short whine and a huge splash, the water soaking us on 'A' mounting. A long hush as we waited for the bomb to explode, but no explosion came. The bomb had scraped the side of the ship and failed to go off. The sound of expelled breathe and a muttered "That was too bloody close" as everybody relaxed.

"BEDOUIN" now completed the turn and headed out of Rombaks Fiord into wider waters, Offot Fiord. Our Captain, Commander J.A. McCoy, a wily tactician, wanted room to manoeuvre and take evasive action at high speed. The aircraft were soon back. A high altitude run along our wake and the bombs were released. Hard over, 25 knots and fire on the roll. That was the order of the day. Our twin 4.7" guns could only elevate to 40° and we wanted 60° at least. We also wanted to save as much high explosive ammunition as we could, so in order to give the impression we mean business, we were firing practice A.A. shells.

Much of the ammunition that had been left after the battle had been used on targets such as the power station in Rombaks Fiord, which had been completely ruined and burnt out. We had stacks of pom-pom and 0.5" machine gun ammunition but, so far, nothing to use it on. What we really required was 4.7" H.E. and semi-armour piercing ammunition. Fresh vegetables were also in short supply and we were hoping that if the supply ship managed to get to us, we might get a goodly supply of all our needs.

The R.F.A. did get to us, hidden in a remote fiord and protected by none other than my old ship, H.M.S. "RESOLUTION". When we got alongside, the first target was to top up with fuel, then ammunition, and then food. Fuel there was aplenty. Ammunition? Well, pom-pom and 0.5" machine gun. No, not even one 4.7" shell. Sorry! On the food side there was plenty of fresh meat, even some fresh spuds, but no green stuff. Oh yes, there were plenty of tins of

Tribal class destroyers in action, second battle of Narvik. H.M.S. "PUNJABI" in foreground.

dehydrated cabbage, so we had to make do with that, and take on a supply of 'Pom', the dried potato powder.

While taking on our supplies, three aircraft appeared from nowhere. "RESOLUTION" opened fire and there came a plaintive voice over the radio-phone to the effect of "Don't you recognise your own bloody aircraft?". They were three from the "ARK ROYAL", (even though the Germans had sunk her about three times already. Well, they said they had, but we knew better).

On finishing fuelling and storing, it was back to Offot Fiord again. This time we would be looking for targets ashore about which we had received from our Norwegian friends, some very good information. According to the current information, the Germans had been hard at work storing munitions in all sorts of places, from churches to private homes.

Nothing untoward happened on the way up Offot Fiord and slowing down as we neared the entrance to Rombaks Fiord, we passed the Polish destroyer "GROM" on our port side. "BEDOUIN" had hardly got through the entrance when a German bomber passed overhead. Within a minute there came one almighty explosion and at once we made one of the smartest and fastest turns ever and steamed out of Rombaks and into Offot Fiord. "GROM" had disappeared. She had, we heard later, been hit by a stick of three bombs. All we could see was a huge black cloud of smoke, slowly rising.

H.M.S. "FAULKNER" and rescue boats.

"FAULKNER", carrying the Captain (D) came rushing across to join us and as the smoke finally lifted, we could see some movement among the figures in the water. Down went our boats and away they went to look for survivors. From the upper deck we could see them lifting the bodies from the ever widening patch of thick black oil. When it appeared that there were no more living or dead in that black patch, the boats came back to the ship and both survivors and expired were brought on board.

Some came aboard unharmed, but shocked. Others had a multitude of injuries, broken limbs, bodies torn with shrapnel from the exploding bombs, all soaked with furnace fuel oil into which was blending the blood from their wounds. A pitiable sight indeed.

"RESOLUTION" had arrived by now, so "BEDOUIN" and "FAULKNER" went alongside her to transfer the dead and wounded. After all, she had a proper operating theatre and a large sick bay and could attend to the "GROM's" survivors better than we destroyers could. During the transfer I could see some of the lads I had been with once and I was not forgotten by Pedlar Palmer who, seeing me, said "And what the bloody hell are you doing there?"

H.M.S. "ENTERPRISE" and H.M.S. "BEDOUIN" boats picking up survivors.

"GROM" survivors being brought abroad H.M.S. "BEDOUIN".

It now became the regular thing to be chased up and down Offot Fiord by enemy planes, who always appeared at the change of watches and just a regularly, for those planes to turn nasty and try to lay eggs on us. At first, the usual stick was three, then it increased to five and sometimes a stick of eight bombs were dropped where we should have been.

At this stage, "BEDOUIN" only had 'B' guns crew closed up and that was the only gun used, it being the best positioned gun in those circumstances. The Gunnery Officer would get on the top of the director tower and lay on his back with a pair of binoculars and watch for when the plane dropped its bombs, shouting the information to the Captain, who then took the necessary avoiding action, which usually meant a hard over to either port or starboard at 25 knots.

At one stage in this bombing campaign by the Boche, the Captain took "BEDOUIN" into an inlet off Offot Fiord and anchored close to the shore, but with a clear run both forward and astern. The anchor cable was then broken at the slip and the detached part connected to a steel wire rope, which in turn was attached to a danbuoy. In effect, we had most of the anchor cable inboard and about a shackle in the water with the anchor on the end.

Second battle of Narvik. German destroyer which ran aground attempting to escape and which torpedoed H.M.S. "ESKIMO".

It did not take long for 'Snoopy' to find us. A sitting target he must have thought, for in he came, but we were ready. The cable was slipped and the engines were going full astern before he released his bombs. As a result, the two bombs he dropped landed one on the shore line and one in the water, close enough to splash us a bit, but not close enough to do any harm. Casualties? Yes. Two seagulls! Unfortunately, we lost our anchor.

Steaming out into the fiord, we waited for the plane to return to the attack. It was not long coming. This time he dropped a stick of five bombs. A sharp turn and a pair of practice round fired as a gesture and the ship straightened up and reduced speed until the nest try. Then a turn in the opposite direction with the same result, watching the bombs follow our wake to where we should have been. This sort of manoeuvring went on until the enemy plane had run out of things to drop on us, when he went home for a rest.

In the middle of all this playing tag with unfriendly aircraft, "BEDOUIN" received a message to proceed to Haarstad and there pick up a detachment of Guards. (I am not sure, but I think they were the Coldstream Guards). There were some 200 of them, in full battle kit and the object of the exercise was to erase a German position of 35 men and one machine gun. Our friendly Norwegian allies had thoughtfully provided some fishing vessels with which the troops would be transferred to the shore.

Arriving at the point where the landing was to have taken place, the Major in command of the Guards went into conference with our Captain. I was on the bridge at the time and heard all that went on. First the Major found fault with his 'landing craft'. He was politely told that was all that was available. Objection by Major, they would be too exposed on those vessels. Our Captain, we will give you covering fire. In any case, once the Major had got his troops ashore they would be exposed anyway. Still the Major hummed and hawed. Our Captain then, very politely, asked if the Major intended to make a landing or not, and if not, then he, the Captain of H.M.S. "BEDOUIN", would return them to Haarstad and return to this spot and blow the Germans and their machine gun sky high.

Back to Haarstad we went, unloaded the troops and then made our way back to where the landing should have taken place. A word with our Norwegian friends and over went a salvo of H.E. shells. Back came the report from our friendly spies that all was well, there were no Germans to worry about.

In the midst of all the activity, "BEDOUIN" entered Narvik Fiord and in the company of a cruiser and other destroyers, sighted a troop carrying aircraft. it was heading toward Narvik and flying low, well within the range of our close range weapons and as all the other ships were firing at the aircraft, "BEDOUIN" joined in with her pom-poms. I am positive I saw a number of those two pounder shells strike the aircraft from nose to tail. Later a target was pointed out to "BEDOUIN" and we were told to hit it. We opened fire and soon, from the target point in the centre of Narvik, a black column of smoke rose into the air.

The cruiser which was present had, at an earlier date, received a direct hit with a bomb on her 'B' turret. Her Captain edged his ship close to "BEDOUIN" and then came aboard and up to the bridge, where he was greeted by our Captain. Remarking on the column of smoke created by our bombardment, the cruiser Captain said, "I'm going to call that Bez's Beacon". Our Captain was called by that name by fellow officers and higher ranks who knew him well.

Moving into Rombaks Fiord, which by now had been christened 'Bomb Racks' Fiord by us, we received information from our usual source, that the Germans had stored ammunition in one of the houses. Our informant came aboard to point out the target, but warned that the houses near to the target were occupied by innocent families. The Captain decided to go in as close as possible, risking getting hurt in the meantime, and give the pom-poms a chance to loose off some of their plentiful ammunition.

The target proved to be rather difficult, being close behind another house. Taking careful aim, they loosed off a few rounds, but spotted someone coming out of the house making frantic signals. Horrified, they realised that they had started to shoot up the wrong house.

Our friends were told to get their people out of that house, or at least get out any casualties and we would take them to the hospital at Haarstad. The Germans, now alerted, promptly took a hand in things and made threats to the Norwegians. A shot in their direction made them think again. As the casualties were being brought down to the shore, "BEDOUIN's" gunners opened up again, this time hitting the right target.

Once again, as the Norwegians loaded their wounded into boats and started to move away from the shore and toward us, the Germans tried to interfere, this time it was a heavy machine gun near the waters edge, which until now had not been seen by us. They ordered the Norwegians back or be shot, and fired a short burst. Target promptly shifted to machine gun post, and quickly wiped out.

Now we had to run the gauntlet. Among the passengers we now had and safely berthed in the Wardroom were a pregnant woman with an injured knee, another woman who had collected a bullet from the Hun, a mother and her two children, all of whom had received wounds of some kind though not severe, a mother and baby and several men, mostly coming as escorts for the women and children.

"BEDOUIN's" nose had barely passed through the entrance of Rombaks Fiord when the attacks from the air began. This had now become a high speed chase all the way down Offot Fiord. The enemy aircraft were really trying to put the pressure on and dropping sticks of up to eight bombs in their efforts to nail us. "BEDOUIN" was heeling over at 25 knots or more, one could hear the whine of the turbines rising and falling as speed was increased or decreased. In the Wardroom the women and children were screaming with every move made, literally becoming hysterical as the ship heeled first one way and then the other and added to that the thud of exploding bombs close by as we turned out of the way.

This had been the most determined assault we had encountered yet, but just as suddenly as it started, so did it cease. Reassuring passengers that all was well turned out to be difficult, but they calmed eventually. At Haarstad we rapidly ferried them ashore to the hospital, to return to the trouble spot once more. That whole episode must have been a very bad nightmare for those women and children.

It must be remembered that Narvik is some 250 miles inside the Arctic Circle and that the spring thaws begin about mid April, and the hours of daylight quickly grow longer and longer as May approaches. So, by the end of April there is almost 24 hours of daylight. In these conditions, the enemy aircraft were able to keep up an almost round the clock bombardment of ships and any land forces in the area. We, trying to operate in these Northern climes, had seen the thaw begin and the snow covered landscape slowly emerge from its covering of white.

Earlier in this narrative, I had mentioned the fact that among the stores we managed to get were tins of dehydrated cabbage. Eventually these tins had to be issued to the messes. With the usual good graces of the Royal Victualling Yard, these had come with no instructions as to how much dehydrated cabbage needed to be used for a fixed number of persons. There being 21 in my mess and nobody knowing quite how much to use, somebody said tip the lot into a bucket of water and see.

We did just that and then left the bucket out of sight overnight. In the morning, looking at the bucket, we found enough cabbage to feed the whole ship's company, if not more. There was cabbage everywhere. Result, cabbage was on the menu for days after, for dinner and supper.

It was now May and we seemed to have acquired a newsreel cameraman. "BEDOUIN" had barely started to steam toward the seaward end of Offot Fiord when the enemy aircraft pounced. The old routine started up again, 25 knots, hard aport, another shower of bombs missed, then hard a'starboard, missed again. I had taken over on the bridge to do my stint of all round look-out/lifebuoy sentry/depth charge dropper all rolled into one and had been watching the antics intently. Then came this one determined pilot. Our speed went up to 26 knots and we did a hard a'starboard. I watched the bombs falling in our wake as we turned and then passed by our rapidly receding stern. I counted a stick of thirteen bombs. (About three weeks later, I watched that scene again in a cinema in Glasgow).

Our time had come for us to return to Blighty. It was now the middle of May and the news coming in from the Continent was not good. The situation in Norway was grim as well. Here, obviously, the Germans had gained the advantage by their sudden simultaneous taking of the main strategic ports, towns and bases on April 4th, 1940. In France they had advanced round the unguarded end of the Maginot Line and had burst through Belgium. However, "BEDOUIN" was to return to Glasgow for a short tidy up.

The first part of the journey home was not without incident. Having gone down the Vest Fiord at speed and turned westward after clearing the southernmost part of the Lofoten Islands, there appeared on the horizon what looked like a large warship, heavy cruiser or battleship. With about 50 rounds of S.A.P. left we went into action stations and then came a recognition signal. The 'enemy' turned out to be the 1917 light cruiser H.M.S. "CAIRO" and she had been in the shadow of a large dark cloud, which appeared to make her seem to be a large warship. Relief all round.

The second incident came soon after. Knowing the risk a single ship has to take, "BEDOUIN" had cracked on the speed and was now doing a steady 25 knots. I had the afternoon watch and, having done my turn on the bridge, was now on the Quarterdeck doing the normal job of depth charge crew cum stern lookout cum lifebuoy sentry.

There was a fair wind and the sea had become choppy. Combined with the speed, this made for sudden lurches every so often. While waiting for my relief to show up, the time then just about 15.55, the Gunnery Officer came up from the Wardroom, fully togged up in cold weather gear and about to take over the 1st Dog Watch on the bridge. As he turned to go along the upper deck, the ship gave one of those sudden lurches and catching Guns off balance threw him against the guard-rail, which caused him to fall over the top and into the sea.

Seeing what happened, I pressed the lifebuoy alarm and let a lifebuoy go. I reported to the bridge, stating who it was in the sea. I had seen Guns vanish astern and had not given him much hope. The water around these coasts are icy cold at all times. The only hope seemed to be that he would float in the gear he was wearing.

The ship had gone into a tight 180° turn and was combing its own wake. The sea boat had been manned and was swung out ready to drop. With everybody available on the upper deck and gun decks scouring the sea, it was hoped that Guns wound soon be found. Our prayers were answered, we had found the tiny dot in the ocean and it took very little time after that for him to be brought back aboard.

Guns' first comment on getting aboard was "I never expected to see you lot again". With sea boat hoisted, the bows were pointed once more toward home. Guns did not seem to be very perturbed about his experience, or perhaps he would not let himself be worried, for all he did was to laugh at himself for going over the side.

On our arrival in the shipyard in Glasgow we were informed that we would be there for about ten days and leave would be given. On my arrival home I was greeted by the sight of my mother out in the garden. I gathered that after my flying visit she had regained her senses and improved rapidly and was now convalescing. She had heard on the radio where we had been.

A few days leave soon goes by, but I was able to visit my sister and brother in their evacuation billets in Horsmonden, Kent. The situation in France had become very serious and some of our forces had been evacuated from various points along the French coast. I heard also that Roy, who had gone to Lee-on-Solent, had been shot down and seriously wounded and was in the Southern Hospital,

Bexley. I learned more about that later when I saw him after he had left hospital.

Leave had ended and the ship had been prepared for sea again, our destination was Scapa. On arrival we had expected to be sent to where all the trouble was, off the beaches of France, but that was not to be. Instead we got the job of escorting an Isle of Man ferry turned troopship to Iceland. There were several of these trips, all done at 22 knots. It did seem that having had our fill in Norway, we were to be spared any more aggro for the time being and kept as far as possible from the beaches at Dunkirk.

This seemed to be a quiet time and once we were sent somewhere south, but out in the Atlantic, but what for I do not know. Returning we were some 400 miles west of the Irish coast when a small sail appeared. Approaching it with great caution, for it was known that U-Boats used things like that for bait to bring a ship within their sights, it turned out to be a loaded lifeboat from a Greek ship that had been sunk recently.

Very slowly we eased toward the boat, our Asdic gear making an all round sweep sometimes transmitting and sometimes listening on hydrophone for propeller noises. As the whole area seemed to be clear of any lurking U-Boats, the lifeboat was given the all clear to come alongside.

There were thirteen men in that small boat, one of them being the Captain of the torpedoed ship. Questioning brought forth the information that these men had been in this boat for ten days and that the U-Boat Captain had given them some supplies and cigarettes and told them land was not far away and pointed westward. Yes! There was land in that direction, only it just happened to be about 3,000 miles that way. The spot where we picked them up was 400 miles west of Ireland and they were going westward.

Most of the survivors were in not too bad a state, although the Captain wanted medical attention. We found out too, that there had been another boat, but the two boats had become separated during the first night and the other boat, in the charge of the first officer had not been sighted since.

In the usual practice of the sea, the survivors were treated like royalty. They were given clothing from members of the ship's company and being spread round the messes, fared well for food. One of these lads, an American negro, had arrived on board minus footwear, so he received a pair of boots from somebody. Yes, he said, they fitted well. The next day however, he was seen standing by the funnel, looking somewhat pained and moving his weight from one foot to the other. When asked if the boots were too tight, he replied, "Dem boots is okay. It's ma feet what's too big".

Leaving the empty lifeboat slowly settling in the water, "BEDOUIN" headed for the nearest port in which the merchant seamen could be landed and duly taken care of. That port, Liverpool. A couple of days later, on entering the mouth of the Mersey, speed had to be reduced to a minimum. Along the course of the buoyed fairway, wrecks of ships abounded. It looked like a graveyard of ships. Not far out of Liverpool, the Asdic operator picked up an echo. The echo was classified as a submarine contact and depth charge stations closed up. The ship's speed at this moment had come down to 6 knots, but as the contact seemed so positive, a depth charge attack was mounted.

With little room to manoeuvre in went "BEDOUIN", dropping a full pattern set at 30 feet. The minimum speed required for this pattern should have been 12 knots, but as the depth charges rolled over the stern and were fired from the throwers either side the speed had barely reached the smallest fraction above 6 knots. The result, as the charges exploded almost under our stern, the whole ship shook and the stern lifted bodily.

So much for that, but a swift inspection showed no structural damage nor any leaks. The mortifying part was that we had actually attacked a wreck which had been just at the edge of the dredged channel.

As the ship had now become due for a boiler clean, we all thought it might be the chance for a couple of days leave. Then came the news that a floating dock had arrived at Scapa and been moored at Lyness and was now waiting for the first customer. Groans and the betting was that we would be the first in the dock. As we had left Liverpool immediately the survivors had been put ashore and were now well up the Irish sea, it had been noticed that the steering did not come quite up to standard. Obviously the depth charges had caused some damage to the rudder itself.

As had been predicted by us all, the signal came shortly before entering Scapa. 'Proceed into floating dock for boiler clean and overhaul'. Moans and groans from all and sundry. However, what was to be had to be and into the floating dock went "BEDOUIN", although not without a last show of defiance, she rammed the dock catwalk, though not causing any damage to either ship or dock.

When the dock had lifted out of the water, the damage to the rudder could be seen. There had been a chunk torn off the rudder which had impaired its operation. The dockyard maties soon fixed that by cleaning up the ragged edge and rivetting on a fresh piece of plate. Thus the rudder became whole again, but for how long?

Once out of the dock, it was back to the old grind once more. Among the many antics came one operation that might have been a resounding success if we had had the full co-operation of the R.A.F.

This operation entailed a force of destroyers, under the wing of a cruiser, to enter a fiord a short distance from Stavanger where the enemy had established a dive bomber base. At the appropriate time, the R.A.F. were to bomb the airfield and keep on bombing it in order to keep the dive-bombers grounded while the tiny force of destroyers sailed up the fiord, blowing everything of importance to bits. Meanwhile the cruiser would be keeping a sharp watch at the entrance for any enemy forces. Two other destroyers loaded with mines were, at the same time, to lay their mines in the shipping lanes.

Unfortunately, this operation had been timed rather hastily and at an inappropriate time, there still being long daylight hours, with only about three or less hours of complete darkness and darkness was indeed a necessity for this kind of job.

Everything had been settled, the R.A.F. were going to play their part, so the Force set off from Scapa, steaming at 28 knots. Naturally, everybody became tense and anxious for darkness to fall on our scheme. The Force had actually sighted the Norwegian coast when, from out of the blue, came the message 'The R.A.F. cannot play tonight, they have other commitments and not enough aircraft.' For a time we all wondered. Then came the message from the C. in C. that it was up to the discretion of the Senior Officer whether we should go ahead as planned or call the whole thing off. Discretion was the operative word, so the whole thing was called off and doing a smart 180° turn, the Force set off for Scapa at a modest 30 knots.

On the lighter side, there was that radio programme called 'Forces Favourites' which usually came on the air at about 08.00. On this particular morning one of the first requests came from a pair of matelots. The young lady announcer innocently said, "The next request comes from two sailors in 'Rose Cottage' Royal Naval Hospital. Their request is for 'There's a tear in my eye and I'm wondering why'". Well, naturally everyone fell about laughing their heads off. The explanation is that 'Rose Cottage' was the name given to the ward kept apart from the others for C.D.A. cases (venereal disease).

Then, of course, there was that other comedian 'Lord Haw Haw'. He seemed to know where every ship of the Fleet was, where it was going and how many times Jerry had sunk it. "BEDOUIN" came in for his attention too. Come to think of it, I am sure now that the overnight stay we had at Londonderry must have been to give that man something to talk about, knowing that the Republic of Ireland was a nest of German spies.

At the beginning of September, "BEDOUIN" joined a force of destroyers at Rosyth. A day or so later we were all ordered out on exercises. There were two sub-divisions, one led by the Flotilla Leader, H.M.S. "SOMALI", and the other by "BEDOUIN". Steaming out to the mouth of the Forth, the two sub-divisions engaged in a game of high speed manoeuvring between May Island and the Bass Rock. While doing these somewhat dangerous operations of the Grid Movement, which meant crossing and recrossing each others paths, turning into line at high speed, turning into line abreast and changing positions, all a great strain on the ships and especially their rudders, "BEDOUIN's" steering started to become a bit erratic, eventually not giving the tight turning required for these particular movements.

"BEDOUIN" excused herself and became a spectator until the Leader gave the order 'Leaders and Half Leaders full ahead and race for Rosyth'. Just the job, for "BEDOUIN" won that with ease.

Now being unable to take part in any operations because of our steering problem, "BEDOUIN" tied up to a jetty. But not for long. There came a call for a sea search and rescue. A Wellington bomber had been badly mauled in a raid and had ditched in the North Sea somewhere off the Dogger Bank. "BEDOUIN" was the one called on to do the search and possible rescue.

The weather, as usual, was no help for this mission. A gale was now blowing and battling south through it, eventually reached the search area. Here there was help in the form of a Coastal Command aircraft, whose job was to frighten off any unwelcome intruders, as well as help in the search. We did see one of the enemy, a Heinkel 115 float plane, probably looking for the same people as we were.

An aircraft dinghy is not an easy thing to find. They may be a bright red, but when you are hunting for something about the size of a large dining room table and the sea is throwing you all over the place, plus being about 20 to 30 feet high, then the task is one of hit or miss. there were no search and rescue beacons in those days and rarely a smoke flare.

Luck was on our side. The accompanying plane spotted a raft and dropped a smoke flare close by, then kept circling and diving over the spot. Making towards it, the masthead lookout saw the smoke flare and pointed out the direction. Soon the raft hove into sight and by backing and filling, got the raft on our lee side and then managing to secure it, brought out the two forms that lay in it.

One of the air crew had died on the raft and the other soon would have done had "BEDOUIN" arrived any later. As it was, that lad lay in the Sick Bay throughout the passage home to base, but he did give us the information needed to tell the sorry tale to relatives. When the plane had crashed, all five of the crew had escaped, but one died soon after and they had to ditch his body. Then, having not been picked up in the first couple of days, the Pilot, weakening rapidly, slid over the side and was washed away. The other member also got washed away when his hold on a lifeline loosened and he let go. That left just the two we had picked up.

A signal had been sent on ahead about the rescue, but as we started on the return journey we encountered a Norwegian fishing vessel sailing in the general direction of Britain. An interception was made and, although expecting something like Nazi spies trying out their luck, the great surprise was that there were two crew and both were Norwegians and they had some information which might prove to be useful.

Bringing them aboard, the Captain thought it a good idea to try to salvage the fishing vessel. So up it came on a set of davits that had no boat at that time and off we sailed into the gloom.

The Norwegians said it would not work, but it did, that is, until one mighty big sea caught the vessel under the keel and lifted it up. As the wave subsided so down came the fishing vessel so heavily that it broke free of the boats falls, hit the ship's side and, mortally wounded, fell into the sea and slowly sank in our wake.

The arrival at Rosyth tended to be rather solemn. The R.A.F. came aboard and took charge of the body and the survivor. He got a cheer from us and good wishes for the future. The body, now in a coffin, left with a certain amount of ceremony and with the thanks of the R.A.F. for bringing home the body. Then it was back to lying alongside the wall.

For a time "BEDOUIN" lay alongside the wall ahead of some S.N.S.O. vessels, but then came the request to move to a certain spot on the wall. Now comes the funny bit. Right in the middle of the part of the jetty where "BEDOUIN" had been told to move to lay one of the S.N.S.O. vessels, quite a small vessel in reality, but big enough to stop us getting alongside.

Again, being on the bridge at the right time, I saw and heard all that passed. Our Captain, "Ship ahoy! Captain, would you please move your ship?". No answer. Again. "Captain, will you please move your ship?". Still no answer. And now. "Captain! Move your ship!". A head sporting a pair of bleary eyes, momentarily popped round and open door, then rapidly disappeared. But still no answer from that ship's Captain. Finally, in exasperation, "Captain! Move your f***ing ship!". That brought forth a very hasty response and within minutes the S.N.S.O. carrier had moved out of the way. The explanation, well, it was Sunday.

Through all this, the Germans were trying to blow London and several other cities to bits, with little success, but it had become known to all and sundry that there had been some heavy casualties in the cities bombed. Now we all had another worry on our hands and minds, our relatives and friends at home. Many were the quiet prayers said for the salvation of our loved ones. When the news came through about the heaviest loss the Hun had suffered in one day, it was three hearty cheers and serve the Hun right.

October 1940. "BEDOUIN" tied up and useless for any daring operation due to steering difficulties. Weather deteriorating. Dive bombers active in the Straits of Dover and E-Boats active all along the south coast. "BEDOUIN" must of necessity go into dock. Problem suddenly solved. "BEDOUIN" is to proceed to Southampton for docking in Southern Railway Old Docks. Hip, Hip, Hooray!

The original route given for the trip to Southampton would have been down the east coast, through the Straits of Dover and thence down the Channel to Southampton. All in authority were well aware of the danger of that route and the increased danger there would be if "BEDOUIN" sailed that route with her steering troubles. It was then that they decided that "BEDOUIN" would sail the up and over route, north to the Orkneys, through the Pentland Firth, along the north coast of Scotland to Cape Wrath, then down through the Minches, Irish Sea, into and up the Channel.

Leaving Rosyth, "BEDOUIN" proceeded north at 20 knots, doing the usual zig-zag en route and keeping that speed until we were in the Minches, when speed was increased to 25 knots. Here we found out just how much trouble we were in.

We met a convoy heading north and we had to take the avoiding action. "Starboard twenty" came the order, being repeated by the helmsman, then the words "Twenty of starboard wheel on, sir". The ship should have been heeling over by now and turning rapidly to starboard. Not so, she kept on a steady course. It made no difference with the wheel hard over to starboard. In a flash came the order, "Stop starboard. Full astern starboard". As this was done the ship swung round to the course intended, westerly.

The use of the wheel was tried when attempting to return to the original course, with the same results as before. So it came down to steering by main engines. A force 8 gale was blowing in the Irish Sea when we came clear of the Minches, but speed now increased to 28 knots. As one can imagine, in these conditions, keeping a steady course became more and more difficult, as the motion of the ship showed.

On reaching the Lizard, the weather worsened and "BEDOUIN" turned up the Channel with a full gale force 9 blowing from the southwest. Speed also increased to 32 knots and with a following sea, did she roll! We were closed up at all night action stations, in case we met any stray E-Boats, not that they were likely to be out in such weather.

As I was now a member of the Tubes Crew I, like the rest, spent the night huddled in the shelter of the engine room hatches cover, with the telephone dangling from my neck. Occasionally we changed places temporarily to go and fetch hot cocoa from the galley. The night was pitch black and all we could see were the white crests of the waves as they rose and then broke, the spray being whipped by the wind into our faces every time we poked our noses out of the shelter.

When daylight finally illuminated the scene, we were steaming at about 14 knots and were passing St Catherine's Lighthouse on the Isle of Wight. Assistance had been called for, we could never have entered Portsmouth Harbour unassisted. The wind had died down a little, but we were still wallowing in huge waves until we reached the comparative shelter of the Island off Ventnor and under the shadow of St Boniface Down. It was after passing Sandown Bay that we picked up the tugs and completed the rest of the journey in their good care.

Our berth, a buoy up in the Trot where we were close to the Ammunition Store. A lighter came alongside and we commenced de-ammunitioning the ship. This was the fastest de-ammunitioning I have ever known. Battle bowlers had to be worn at all times when on the upper deck, mainly due to the over activity of the Hun planes.

About the time we were half way through the de-ammunitioning, over came an Me.110 and, shooting down a barrage balloon, he tried to do the Victory Roll, only to be pounced upon and shot down himself.

As soon as the de-ammunitioning had been completed, the tugs returned, tied up alongside and took us off out of Portsmouth Harbour, up the Solent and Southampton Water, to the berth alongside the dry dock in which "BEDOUIN" would be placed the next day.

That night, local leave was given until midnight. As many as possible went ashore, even if only to stretch legs, but, of course, the only thing most wanted to stretch were their arms over the bar of the nearest pub. At that time Southampton had not received much in the way of air raid damage, all that came later. It did however, give those of us who went ashore that night the chance to find out the exact whereabouts of the main railway station. It also allowed us to find out the times of the trains to and from Waterloo. These times could only really be trusted to be anywhere near right if there had been no air raids in the vicinity.

Returning from shore that night, I found myself strolling along behind a line of six of the lads. Suddenly, from out of the shadows, leapt two Squaddies, then the shout "Halt! who goes there?". Back came the answer, "Six matelots - all pissed!". "Advance six matelots all pissed" called back our friendly soldier and as they all began to move forward he added, "One at a time". "Oh no, not one at a time, we'll all fall over", answered the merry matelots. Grinning broadly, the sentry answered "Okay, have it your own way" and as they passed him, adding "Goodnight mates".

The next morning "BEDOUIN" went into dry dock early and once settled and the dock pumped out, the first leave party were ready to step ashore, once leave passes had been dished out.

There are many things to attend to when going into dry dock and not least that of getting a decent electric shore supply and we torpedo men had the job of connecting the shore supply to our switchboard via shore cables. While doing this, one of the dockyard workers came along and said "How the bloody hell did you manage to make it here?". "Why?" came the quite natural query. "Look at that" said the dockie, pointing to the stern. On looking, it was quite plain what he meant. Where the rudder should have been, there hung only the pintle and a couple of spikes of metal. To say we had steering problems was puttting it mildly.

If I remember correctly I went on leave with the first party. The train for Waterloo left at 11.30 and, as it was wartime, stopped at extra stations along the line. A speed restriction had been imposed when there were air raid warnings given and it was this that decided the time of arrival at our destinations, or not.

This day the train had a fairly good run as far as Woking, then the speed restrictions came into play. I know not how many times that train started to gain speed, only to be slowed down almost immediately. For us passengers it was most frustrating. Finally the train drew to a halt at Wimbledon and it was "All out". The line had been cut somewhere near Vauxhall, so buses were laid on. The line between Waterloo Junction and London Bridge had also been put out of operation, some filthy Hun had knocked down a bridge. So it had to be Victoria and hope for the best and a train from there.

Where my parents lived just happened to be in the no-mans land between the main London barrage and the outer rings of anti-aircraft defences, right in the path of any nervous Hun who thought to get rid of his load quick and get home to supper.

Hence, I soon got used to the sounds of bombs whistling down, sometimes far off, sometimes too close for comfort. This still did not deter me from making a nightly visit to my current girl friend, cycling like mad in the blackout.

Each night I got information from my father on the state of the railway from home to Waterloo and Charing Cross and back again. the day I was due to return off leave, happened to be at that period when there had been a slackening off of raids on London and the lines were clear into and out of London.

The down train from Waterloo to Southampton left on time and arrived fairly well to time, when accounting for the numerous slowings for track repair work. Hence, a return to the ship on time. None of us knew it at the time, but our new 1st Lieutenant had arrived on the same train, so we would have been in the clear even if the train had arrived late. There is a funny story attached to that as well. It concerned two members of the engine room department who lived in close proximity and were, therefore, great chums.

These two gents, both Stokers, lived in the Canterbury area and had, so it seems, missed the train which would have got them to Waterloo in time to connect with the Southampton train. When brought before the 1st Lieutenant for being absent over leave, their excuse was that the train they should have caught had run late and they just missed the Southampton train at Waterloo. Number One then asked, out of the blue, where they lived and what time was the train they purported to have caught. Having answered the question Jimmy, the One, looked at them, then slowly said "Now that's funny. I caught that train and it was on time. What part of the train did you catch?". Well, no answer, Number One also came from the Canterbury area.

During this refit certain alterations had to be made. First, 'X' gun mounting had to be removed and a twin 4" HA/LA mounting put in it's place. This was to perk up our anti-aircraft defences. Also for firing star shell. Oerlikon 20mm guns were also fitted on either wing of the flag deck under the bridge, and on 'X' gun deck. A radar cabin had to be built on the flag deck, on the centre line, directly under the bridge so that it appeared to be part of the bridge structure. On the top of the foremast went the radar scanner.

To offset all this extra weight being placed well above the water line, something had to be moved. The depth charge throwers came down from 'X' gun deck on to the upper deck, the after funnel shortened by two feet and, to give an all round firing arc for the new 4" gun, the mainmast was shortened. Then, 40 tons (I think), of pig iron ingots were placed into the boiler rooms bilges.

While all this was going on, we crew members left aboard were doing our little best to help things along. As torpedomen were the electricians in those days, jobs aplenty could be found.

Then one clear, slightly sunny day, from out of the blue came this Me.110, diving at the ship, high and dry in the dock, and it let go three bombs. At that moment I was in the director tower, helping out with some weapon control checks. There came a roar as the plane swooped low over the ship, and zooming upward, disappeared from my sight. Then came three explosions, one on the dockside near the bows, one hitting a pile of wooden sleepers which were near the dockside and on a level with the bridge of the ship, and the third just short of the docks at our stern.

None of these bombs caused any damage to either ship or dock, but two dockyard workmen who took shelter under the sleeper stack were killed.

Then Lord "Haw Haw" chipped in with his party piece. Breakfast time and the radio switched on. We used to tune in to "Jairmany calling" as Haw Haw used to say, and this particular morning was no different, except for the message. We heard "Jairmany calling. Jairmany calling. All you members of the "BEDOUIN's" crew, do not return to your ship if you wish to see your wives and families again. We know where you are, and we will destroy you". Of course, we fell about laughing, we couldn't help it. We had so many times heard his threats that we took no notice of his rantings.

Trams used to run everywhere in Southampton in those days, and for Servicemen it was one penny for anywhere you were going. In most cases the conductors refused to take any fares, or give us a ticket if an inspector happened to be around. Various places soon received various names in typical matelot fashion. The people of Southampton did us proud, each in their own way. They were very friendly and helpful.

At last, in November 1940, "BEDOUIN" had finished her refit and was ready to take to the sea again. Now we had to go back into Portsmouth to ammunition ship, then do gun trials on the new 4" gun before setting off back to the war zone. Fully refuelled, "BEDOUIN" slipped down Southampton Water, into the Solent and back into Portsmouth Harbour, where ammunitioning was carried out at high speed, and on completion off to sea for the gun trials. It was dark before those trials were completed.

The Dockyard workmen and other civilian staff were taken off by a harbour launch, and "BEDOUIN" proceeded to seawards, keeping to a maximum of 14 knots so that no wake could be seen either from the air or from any lurking E-Boat. The night was clear and fine, and hardly any pitch or roll.

Passing south of the Isle of Wight, the sound of Rolls Royce engines passed overhead as planes from English airfields went on their way to give back to the enemy some of what they had been giving us. Mingling with the noise of the British planes came the moaning sound of the German aero engine approaching the south coast and going inland.

To the south, where the R.A.F. planes crossed the coast of France, we could see the sky lighting up with the bursting of anti-aircraft fire from the German guns. Along the south coast of England, we watched as the night sky lit up with the glare of flares and the flashes of exploding bombs.

Remembering Lord Haw Haw's words, and looking in the direction of Southampton, all we could see there were flashes of the A.A. guns firing and the almost incessant thud and flash of exploding bombs. Our comment, "Southampton must be getting it tonight". It was, and did it catch it that night, their worst ever bombing raid.

As we slowly moved down the Channel, we could still see where more attacks were being made in a number of isolated spots, but as the morning became lighter, so the raids eased off. Now with first light we were able to crack on the speed a bit, and were soon steaming through the Irish Sea.

Our arrival in Scapa caused some comment for, during the refit, we had seen the ship change colour. From the dark reddish grey "BEDOUIN" had been decked out in, she now sported Cambridge blue and white, the white on all the parts of the ship that would normally be in shadow, the blue where the full daylight struck it. This colour formation had been worked out by the boffins in the camouflage department. For dull and misty weather it worked fine, and even in bright moonlight it was quite difficult to pick out.

Before going further at this point, I have remembered a piece of equipment that had been fitted several months prior to our docking. The devilish device was removed during the refit at Southampton. With dive bombers becoming a menace, ways and means had to be found to combat them. Various ideas had been thought up and discarded as unworkable. As dive bombers usually tried to bomb along the length of a ship, then a device on the stern might just frighten them off. So what came up? A compressed air grenade thrower! The thrower was a long tube just round enough for a grenade to be dropped into it. It could be moved in a circle, or rather a half circle and was positioned above the tiller flat, and down in the tiller flat a high pressure air cylinder was fitted, with a pipe which went up to the thrower.

At the base of the thrower there was a trip, which allowed the air to blow out the grenade. So, in the event of a dive bomber suddenly making a pass at the ship, the bomb thrower would be manned, with one man pointing the mortar at the plane, and the second man pulling the pins out of the hand grenades and popping them into the barrel as fast as he could. In theory, fine, but in practice, we-ell, not quite. The weapon was tried with used tobacco tins partly filled to the weight of a grenade and these worked very well, apart from the fact that they never went very high. The crunch came when a live grenade was tried. Out shot the grenade and dropped into the sea just feet from our stern before exploding. That was the end of that object.

One of the early ventures came soon after our arrival at Scapa. This was a repeat, after a fashion, of the earlier attempt at a raid, which had been called off due to failure of R.A.F. activity. This time there were to be two cruisers, who would patrol to seaward to ward off any intrusion by larger enemy forces, two destroyers stripped for mine laying, and fully loaded, who would lay their high explosive eggs in the main channels, and four Fleet destroyers, and their job was to create a diversion by steaming up the adjacent fiord and shooting up anything and everything that we happened to meet or see.

This time darkness was in our favour, and the forces steamed to the dispersal point without so much as a peep out of the, quite obviously, unsuspecting enemy. The four destroyers slowly slipped into the fiord and crept along the main channel. We knew that we only had a certain time to carry out this raid, otherwise our chances of getting back to Scapa unharmed would be very slight, for we would then have the dive-bombers from Stavanger on our tails.

Then, almost without spotting it, a faint light was reported. It was so faint it could only just be made out. Obviously a ship sliding down the channel to the sea. Came the order to illuminate target with starshell. This must be a ship, it is steaming towards us at about 12 knots. I had been told to go and man the searchlight in the after control position. "BEDOUIN" opened fire on the moving ship, and there appeared to be some answering fire, so the order came to illuminate target by searchlight. I had switched on the light, so all I had to do was open the shutter, but would that shutter open, not on your life. Somehow it had jammed. The cease fire order was given, and everything went back to normal. But what had we been firing at? The answer lay in the Captain's log, which read '00.01 opened fire on darkened island with lighthouse. 00.03 ceased fire. Darkened island with lighthouse sunk.'

Steaming back down the fiord, nothing was met, and for all the noise, it seemed that the Germans were all fast asleep. Rejoining the remainder of the Force, we returned to Scapa, a bit bleary eyed, but happy to be safe.

The Home Fleet had by now been strengthened by the arrival of the battleships "KING GEORGE V", "PRINCE OF WALES, and "ANSON", all coming from the builders yards almost at the same time. These ships were fast, compared with the older ones, even "NELSON" and "RODNEY" could only steam at 23 knots flat out. These new ships were 30 knots plus when they got going.

A new breed of aircraft carriers were appearing on the scene as well. The "VICTORIOUS" was the first, and obviously from the same stable as "ARK ROYAL", but bigger. "BEDOUIN" would see more of those ships later on.

Christmas 1940 saw "BEDOUIN" in Scapa, along with several members of the 6th D.F. The best had to be made of the time we had in harbour, so, as we torpedomen knew that the whaler would be going inshore to collect some Christmas cheer, we thought it would be great fun to take the dinghy, dress up as pirates and waylay the whaler on the way back to the ship. Flour bombs were made ready, and off we went for the piratical act of the day. The only trouble was that the seamen got to know of our plot, and took the second whaler and waylaid us. It was a battle royal for a time, but we torpedomen were overwhelmed and thrown out of our boat and had to swim back to the gangway. Watching from a short distance away, a grey seal showed no apparent surprise at the antics of these silly men, and continued to survey the scene with aloof disdain.

During the refit, there had been one or two changes in the torpedo party. The T.I. had left and the new one, Petty Officer Brian Clowes had taken firm control. We all got on very well with him. One of the other members who had joined our happy throng was Lofty Grattan, A.B. L.T.O.(W). He hailed from Derbyshire, Long Eaton actually, and soon became known as the Long Eaton Liar, on account of the tall stories he used to tell. His favourite saying when relating some adventure in which he had taken part in, when asked what he did, would answer "I shit!"

The new German battleship, "BISMARK", had been doing trials in the Baltic, and this caused a stir among the top brass. Some way had to be devised to keep the ship bottled up in the Baltic if possible. For this to be effective, there would have to be day and night reconnaissance, which again could only be done by aircraft. Nevertheless, there were movements of ships between Scapa and

Iceland, where we had a refuelling base. As often as not, a squadron of ships, mainly destroyers screening a big ship of two, would sail for Iceland, refuel there and then sail off into the Atlantic to a position on longitude 25° west, or sometimes 32° west, and then turn back, returning to Scapa.

With the approaching completion of the last two new battleships, "DUKE OF YORK" and "HOWE", the Home Fleet would be ready for anything. The main worry was that the whereabouts of all the German capital ships were not known. The Hun had become an extremely wily old fox, and he would move ships from one spot to another under the cover of bad weather when reconnaissance aircraft either could not see them, or would be grounded because of bad flying conditions. It therefore remained on the good reporting of our submarines should they have witnessed such a move, or by a daring sweep along hostile shores by fast destroyers attempting to lure out the enemy.

It must also be remembered that in 1941, the U-Boat campaign began to intensify, and merchant ships were being sunk faster than they could be built. Also, the enemy were not very worried what country the ships they sank belonged to. It had become a very worrying time for all concerned. Ships like the "QUEEN MARY" and "QUEEN ELIZABETH" always sailed unescorted, relying on their speed to avoid any submarine attack. It was the very slow ships that needed all the geeing up they could be given that sailed in convoys. "BEDOUIN" sailed with several such slow coach convoys, usually with one of the older battleships sitting right in the middle of the convoy as a protection, of sorts, against attacks from the likes of the "SCHARNHOST" and sister ships that were roaming around.

It was generally accepted that U-Boats could not operate efficiently any further west than longitude 32° west, owing to problems of amount of oil carried and risk involved in attempting to send a supply ship to them. For one thing, the Royal Navy were always on the lookout for suspicious looking ships which might well be German replenishment ships. Therefore, under this assumption, all convoys were escorted to as far as 32° west longitude, and then the escort turned back, or elements such as the Fleet destroyers turned for home.

Arriving at Iceland on one operation, the whole fleet, owing to a bad weather warning, foregathered in Hval Fiord close by Reykjavik. The storm hit at a hurricane force and the destroyers began to drag anchors. All were told to move further into the fiord and anchor in the shelter of an island. This done and with two anchors down, the wind howling down the fiord at a speed of 137 knots, "BEDOUIN" had her main engines turning at 12 knots ahead in order to keep in the correct position in the anchorage.

H.M.S. "BEDOUIN" off Iceland at 30 knots.
Duty Destroyer (Guardship).

There was one thing that was never done usually. That was to leave a depth setting on the depth charges when at sea, they were always kept at safe. There were good reasons for this and very valid reasons for not setting a depth on a charges until an attack on a submarine was imminent. Should the ship be torpedoed and start to sink, those charges would go off and kill or seriously main the survivors.

However, at one time our Jimmy the One ordered that all depth charges be set so that a quick pattern could be loosened off once we had the U-Boat in our sights, then we could set the depth again as we reloaded the throwers and trap. Escorting the "KING GEORGE V" to Iceland, the weather became extremely bad, and visibility severely reduced. The heavy seas came over the iron deck in swamping cascades. It was the First Watch (20.00 to midnight) and I had started the watch on the quarterdeck. At 21.00 I made my way forward, firmly hanging on to the lifeline, and running like mad between breaking seas, and went up to the bridge. Shortly after my arrival, and standing in the bridge wing, binoculars hung round my neck, a perfectly useless weight in that sort of weather, and staring aft, I heard this dull thump of an explosion.

The Officer of the Watch heard it too. He asked what it was. My reply was that we must have lost a depth charge overboard. Big flap. Meantime I had phoned the Quarterdeck and asked the bodies there if they would kindly mind going out into the tempest and informing me if we were short of any depth charges. The answer came back quickly, yes, the one from the starboard thrower had gone.

Informing the Officer of the Watch of the news, Number One, who had arrived on the bridge by then, immediately ordered that all charges be made safe, and to, if possible, reload the starboard thrower. Thereafter, the charges were kept at safe until required. We also discovered that our new disguise had made us all but invisible in that kind of weather.

At the beginning of March 1941, our chance came to take part in what was to be the first combined operation, where we landed Commandos. The whole operation had been very carefully thought out to give us the best chance of success. Many people may have thought of it as a hit and run raid, but this one was to be a hefty wallop and toddle off home.

The object of our attentions was to be the Lofoten Islands, Northern Norway, well known to "BEDOUIN" and her crew as the entrance to Narvik. The whole idea was to sail up the Vest Fiord and do as much damage as possible, especially to the German military machine.

For this operation, two railway ferries which belonged to the L.M.S. Railway had been converted into troopships carrying landing craft. There were four Fleet destroyers in the escort/strike force, all from the 6th D.F. The operation could be a risky one, it all depended on the alertness of the German garrison there. There would be a covering force for our outward and return journeys, the covering force being kept between the strike force and the enemy.

A British submarine was positioned in the Vest Fiord and would contact the convoy as it approached the scene of the raid. So everything had been worked out to the last dot and comma. The attack would start at 05.00, 4th March 1941.

Down on the mess decks, we knew something was in the offing, but not what. That information was given to us by the Captain once we had left Scapa. In actual fact, we called in to the Faeroes to top up with fuel, and that was where we got to know the full story. Picking up the convoy, the four destroyers formed the usual screen around the troopers.

Keeping well to the westward, the strike force steamed northerly, keeping as far as possible from the prying eyes of enemy aircraft. We aboard "BEDOUIN", knowing the area to which we were going, knew that we would have to approach in broad daylight once we had made contact with the submarine.

Bang on time the force arrived at the entrance to Vest Fiord and proceeded up the coast, apparently unnoticed. At the first fish oil factory, the first load of Commandos went ashore in their landing craft, with a destroyer mounting a guard over them. The force carried on up the fiord until all the landing parties had gone ashore.

What a surprise the Germans had that morning. The airfield and the radio station, which were prime targets, were caught literally with their trousers down, none of them had got out of bed when the Commandos leapt in among them. The radio mast was blown up, and the transmitters and receivers destroyed. The airfield wrecked and made difficult to put into operation for some time.

Where the fish oil factories had stood, there now rose black plumes of smoke, and the local populace were clamouring to be taken back to Britain with us. The nearest we saw to an actively belligerent opponent, was a small patrol vessel which poked its nose out of the cover of a fiord further up the Vest Fiord, saw us and promptly hopped back into cover again.

"BEDOUIN" stopped a merchant ship, which disobeyed our order to stop, and which then found itself on the receiving end of some very explosive 4.7" bricks. Having sunk that ship, our attention turned to gathering in the prisoners taken by the Commandos. Among the bunch that were delivered to "BEDOUIN", there were two German matelots. One was a U-Boat submariner, and a rather overbearing ARROGANT, pig-headed swine who thought that his big talk would frighten us. We just laughed at the stupid oaf. The other matelot had been absent over leave, taken into the gentle custody of the German version of the Military Police, and was being brought back for trial and punishment aboard his ship, being shot at dawn. Well, he was laughing, because we had his guards as well.

The sum total that day added up to airfield and radio-communications wrecked, all fish oil factories blown up and burnt, a large number of prisoners, 350 Norwegian volunteers to come to Britain with us and 18,000 tons of shipping sunk.

And now for the return home. We had been at action stations all day long, and the only food we had received all day had been corned beef sandwiches, plus hot tea as many times as possible.

Although the day had been dry, bright and sunny with a cloudless sky, which had made it difficult for an enemy aircraft to approach without being seen, the cold had been severe, well below freezing point. It had been that cold, that a cup of boiling tea froze into a solid mass within five or six minutes. Several times I had been distracted when I had just received a fresh hot cup of tea, had put it down, and when I picked it up to drink, found I had a cup of ice. My tea had been frozen solid.

By late afternoon, and still without any intervention, the prisoners had been brought from shore and those destined for destroyers put aboard and taken below under armed guard. The migratory Norwegians had been taken aboard the troopships and all landing craft hoisted on their davits on the troopers.

Now formed into a convoy once more, the journey home commenced. Steaming at 22 knots, the blazing fish oil factories were fading away in the distance, when the cry suddenly went up "Enemy aircraft". Ironic, because the only aircraft we were likely to see in these parts were the enemy's own. However, the plane may have been in some doubt about the identity of the ships below, because the 'Tribal' class destroyers looked very similar to a class of German destroyers, the 'Maas' class, I believe, so there was no attempted close approach made.

The convoy had by this time neared the entrance of Vest Fiord and that meant unlimited ocean to manoeuvre about in. So, without more ado, we let rip with our new 4" gun. How surprised that pilot must have been when a burst of H.E. went off under his tail. Each destroyer had a go at the plane, which did not wait around to find out who we were. Our fears were that the plane would have reported our position to the bomber bases, and that we would shortly come under heavy attack from dive-bombers and high level bombers very soon, but no such attack happened.

Just prior to sighting the plane, the Force had encountered the local fishing fleet coming in, who had seen the smoke from the burning fish oil factories. They signalled us to stop and then some of the vessels came alongside and offered us as much fresh cod as we wanted in exchange for a tin of tobacco. They got several tins of tobacco on each vessel and we received enough cod to last us a week, having cod three times a day.

Reaching the tail of the Lofotens, the convoy turned westwards, and steamed at 'Best possible speed' to get as far from land as possible, and to where it might be out of the range of the bombers. Our luck held for we saw no sign of the enemy planes which we expected would come.

Our prisoners were allowed on the upper deck for an hour at a time, always under armed guard, and every time that ill-begotten Nazi submariner appeared on deck, he started on about how the mighty German "KREIGSMARINE" would come and catch us, and how all the ships would be sunk and we would all become prisoners of the Third Reich. His travelling companion, the leave-breaking frigate matelot, would shake his head and point to the submariner and then tap his temple.

Then, on 6th March at about 11.30, the submariner spotted a pair of ships, soon recognised to be cruisers, bearing down on us. All his exhortations about him being saved and taken back to Germany, seemed to him to be coming true. In high excitement he yelled out words to the effect that he had told us so, the German navy were here to sink us and rescue him. He seemed nonplussed when nobody took any notice of him or what he said, and continued as if there were no cruisers within hundreds of miles of us.

His next outburst brought forth the comment that if he cared to take a look, a much closer look at the 'German' ships, he would find they were wearing the White Ensign, and if they were enemy ships, why were we not at action stations and busy trying to sink them. Finally the penny dropped, and he shut up.

On our arrival in Scapa, the prisoners had to be transferred to the appropriate authorities, and as is standard practice, the prisoners were blindfolded before being brought on to the upper deck. This move put the submariner in an acute state of funk. When on the upper deck, he really began to fear for his life, and when his turn came to cross the gangway, his nerve finally broke. Going down on his knees he started to tearfully plead for his life, he didn't want to be shot. Hauled to his feet, he left the ship on the end of the G.I.'s boot.

What made this raid all the more important for us was that the morning after the raid, news of the attack on enemy occupied territory was broadcast on all B.B.C. stations. More particularly for the participants in the attack, lay in the allowing of the Ship's companies who had taken part, to write home and tell their families that they had taken part.

When the C. in C. Home Fleet decided to have an exercise with his new, large and fast ships, he took with him some dozen destroyers and the Carrier "VICTORIOUS". He chose a rough and windy day. The object seemed to be the feasibility of the carrier being able to keep it's position in the Fleet and still fly off aircraft. The older carriers had to steam into the wind at full speed to fly off their aircraft. That was just not on when there were so many U-Boats on the loose looking for some such target as a carrier out on its own.

"VICTORIOUS" flew off her planes, into the wind, with the wind on the beam, and with the wind astern. All this meant a lot of punishment for the destroyers, for they had to follow suit, and usually steam faster. The exercise on the escorting destroyers was one of keeping one's feet, which at times meant one foot on the deck and one foot on a bulkhead. At these times the speed was 30 to 33 knots, or perhaps a shade more at times.

It was during one of these spells of high speed, with the sea on the port bow, that I received some slight damage. Dinner had been piped, and I was on my way from the galley to mess with a 'fanny' of boiled spuds in each hand. I had negotiated the passageway as far as the hatch leading down into my mess. As I stepped on to the steel ladder, and went to put my other foot on a lower rung, so the ship hit a big one, and without warning, heeled sharply to starboard. My feet slipped off the ladder and I came to rest with my arms out over the hatch combing, still grasping the two 'fannies' of spuds. Unfortunately, on the way down, I had caught my head on a flood valve casing and gashed open my right eyelid.

Tom Kilbey had come to my aid, putting my feet back on the ladder rungs and then taking the pots of spuds from me, but when he saw me after I had come right down into the mess, he ordered me straight to the Sick Bay. After a temporary patch up, I was told to come back at 14.15 and see the Doctor. I had to have a couple of stitches, and although only a minor operation, all the medical staff were there. One held me and the chair I was sitting in steady, while the other S.B.A. held on to the Doctor while he sewed me up.

At the end of the exercise, when "VICTORIOUS's" aircraft were returning to land on her, I saw a piece of first class professional flying done by a 'Fulmar' pilot. On his run in, when he lowered his wheels, only the port wheel came down. He got the wave off, and circled until all the others had landed, and when he was finally called in, "VICTORIOUS" steamed into the wind at over 30 knots. The pilot brought his plane in and over the flight deck brought his speed down to almost stalling and then dropped very gingerly on to the deck, moved forward a few yards and then slowly sank on to its right side. As far as we could see, there had been no damage to the aircraft whatever, but then, we were not on the carrier to make sure.

The Fleet had put to sea again on another of the offensive/defensive patrols designed to prevent any German capital ship getting out to run wild across the oceans. "BEDOUIN" in the screen got a 'ping', and this developed into an anti-submarine attack. The torpedo party were closed up at depth charge stations, and "BEDOUIN" went in for the first attack. The first pattern was fired.

We torpedomen quickly moved in to reload throwers and trap. At the same time, 'X' guns crew were ordered to man 'Y' mounting and load with S.A.P. and to train on a safe bearing. The guns were loaded and then, as they went to train the mounting, both guns fired.

The result of this, Billy Cook, L.T.O. was blown over the stern, the rest of us on the stern caught the blast from the guns, all of us were deafened and had our hair burned off our necks, eyebrows, and had some form of burns on our faces. I had been knocked flat over the spare charges rack and finished half out through the guard-rails. I found my cap lodged behind the rack.

Having seen Billy Cook disappear over the stern, a lifebuoy had been thrown over, we had replaced the safety bar across the trap, and removed impulse charges from the throwers. Billy, so he told us later, found himself saying goodbye to the ship, and then tried to take off his sea boots. By then the ship had started on her way to pick him up.

A quick look over in the Sick Bay, and all except Billy were pronounced fit, except for being deaf, which ailment wore off after about 24 hours. Bill Cook spent the next three days in the Sick Bay with burns and exposure to overcome, and was lucky that he had no scars from the burns, and like the rest of us, his hair grew again.

In May 1941, "BEDOUIN" and another destroyer "INTREPID", had been detailed to escort a R.F.A. transport ship which, we were told, was loaded with supplies and spare parts and other equipment required for the refit the "RODNEY" was due to have in America. This trip was to be the 'great we just missed it' journey.

Our orders were to escort the transport as far as 32° west and then proceed to Iceland. This little convoy must have started out about the same time that the "BISMARK" broke out of the Baltic. However, despite increasingly bad weather, our little convoy kept an average speed of about 12 knots. "BEDOUIN" and "INTREPID" parted company from the transport late on 24th May, and then proceeded on a course for Hval Fiord, Iceland.

During the course of the last few days, we had been given news of the breakout of the "BISMARK" and of the subsequent sinking of the "HOOD" and damage to the "PRINCE OF WALES". Our thoughts were that if we met up with "BISMARK", we would not stand a chance. Due to the "INTREPID" developing a fault in her condensers, the maximum speed she could do was 20 knots, which left both of us very vulnerable.

On 25th May, we received signals that "BISMARK" had been lost, only her last course and speed were known. That meant she could be anywhere, heading west, south, or even trying to get into one of the French ports.

"BEDOUIN" and "INTREPID" were now plunging along at 18 knots in a gale force 8, and likely to get worse. Commander McCoy gave orders for all night actions stations. At least, in the dark, two lonesome destroyers might have an advantage and manage to get in a surprise torpedo attack. Not that we were that optimistic.

All through that foul night, our 'Bunch of grass' type radar searched all round for any sign of a large stray ship heading in our direction, but no such sign showed on the radar screen, and as morning lightened into full daylight, a great sigh of relief went up all round. It was later that day that signals started coming in that "BISMARK" had been found, and that torpedo attacks had been made by Swordfish aircraft from "ARK ROYAL". The following day, 27th May, the most welcome signal of all came through, the "BISMARK" had been sunk.

The sad ending to the "BISMARK" saga came on the next day, 28th May 1941, when the first total loss to the 6th D.F. happened. "MASHONA" had been trying to find the "BISMARK's" supply ship, and somewhere off the coast of Ireland, had come under attack from enemy planes, and had been sunk.

About three months later, whilst having a few days rest in Scapa, the tubes crew and T.C.O. went across to the destroyer depot ship "MAIDSTONE", for a session on the Torpedo Attack Teacher.

While waiting around for our boat back to "BEDOUIN", after the session had finished, the officer in charge of the Teacher called us into an office and told us there was something he wished to show us. It was a large chart showing the positions and tracks of all ships that had actually been involved in the chase and kill of the "BISMARK", and of other ships in the vicinity. It clearly showed that at midnight on 25th/26th May, "BEDOUIN" and "INTREPID" had been 30 miles from the "BISMARK", but that "BISMARK" had turned away from us, and had thus turned into the path of the Catalina flying boat which spotted her about mid-morning on 26th May.

The powers that be found a new job for the ships of the Home Fleet, now that the Arctic nights had become day. The 24 hours of daylight of the Arctic summer had brought out something else for us to sort out, weather ships. These were ocean going type trawlers, but fitted out with the latest weather and radio equipment, and lurked amid the icebergs and large ice floes in the Arctic wastes, sending back valuable weather information to Germany, much of which helped the Hun to plan his air raids.

Our job was to find these ships and try to capture them, and if not able to make a capture, make sure they went to the bottom. Capture as many crew members as possible, and try for the secret codes and suchlike.

The force usually consisted of four destroyers and one cruiser. Once in the area of operations, namely north of the Jan Mayen Islands to Spitsbergen, and west to Greenland coast and east towards Bear Island and north Russia.

"BEDOUIN" did three of these patrols in all. The first one, with the patrol spread out in line abreast, with each ship 10 miles from the next ship, a whole lot of ocean could be covered, for with the normal visibility at that time of the year, an area of approximately 70 miles across by 30 miles wide, given the visibility range to be 15 miles, could be searched on one leg of the patrol.

In this patrol we sighted a trawler, and giving the signal to the cruiser, went after the trawler at high speed. The trawler spotted us and took off, but then came the neatest bit of gunnery I have ever witnessed. It had become obvious that these weather ships had a fair turn of speed, and it would take a considerable length of time to catch up with it. The cruiser took it upon herself to stop the weathermen's flight. She fired one salvo from her 6" guns, and dropped the shots all bunched up either side of the trawler. Never have I seen such panic either.

The weather ship stopped, and by the time "BEDOUIN" had got alongside her, the seacocks had been opened, the crew were waiting on the upper deck, bags all packed, ready to be taken into custody. That was one of the failures, although it cleared one of the weather spies out of the way.

The second patrol had more success, one weather ship was caught, taken completely by surprise and boarded before the crew had time to ditch or destroy the codes and other information required by the powers that be. Also we had increased our own number of weather ships by the total of one. This ship had been caught by the destroyer at the starboard end of the line.

It is hard to describe what the wastes of the Arctic are really like, there is a certain air of solemn and somewhat overwhelming grandeur. It reminds me of entering one of the great cathedrals when they are empty of people, with the exception that the silence of the Arctic has just that hint of the ominous about it.

The magnificence of the great icebergs as they pass by, twisted into fantastic shapes as they slowly melt in the Arctic sun. The many different hues of the bergs, and the rainbow effect as the sun catches them, has to be seen to believe it. The large flat floes, some big enough to hold half a dozen Wembley's with some left over for the Kop, float solemnly by, the waves breaking at their base, but these are to be avoided at all cost.

Often icebergs had a huge underhang protruding out from the sides under water which, as the "TITANIC" found out, can be very dangerous. So, a safe distance always had to be kept from them. Strangely enough, the icebergs, although many in number, were all spaced well apart, leaving broad channels between them.

The sinking or capture of these weather ships were never announced or publicly admitted, we merely made a good half dozen of them vanish off the face of the earth. Keeping the enemy guessing was the name of the game. But there was one mysterious object which needs mention. On one of these operations, we found a large mooring buoy floating amidst the ice floes, so what was that doing there?

Back in Scapa, early in July 1941, "BEDOUIN" had prepared two torpedoes for a practice firing, using a cruiser as the target. We were to slip and proceed into the Flow at 08.00 and complete firing by 09.00. That morning at 07.30 it started to snow, and came on to a blizzard, snow so thick it was like a blanket around you. However we proceeded as planned, and picked up our target by using our A/S gear. Although we could see no sign of the cruiser through the blinding snow, we fired our two 'kippers', and then turned to follow them, for we had to pick them up at the end of their run, they had blowing heads fitted, and would be giving off smoke from the flares they carried in the heads.

Just as suddenly as it had started, the snow stopped, and by the time we had recovered our two fish and returned to our berth at Lyness, about 10.30, the sun was shining brightly and all trace of the snow had disappeared. The cruiser had signalled to us that we had scored with both fish and they were glad they weren't the enemy if we did that every time.

Earlier in the year, "BEDOUIN" had gone to Rosyth for a boiler clean and a few days leave had been granted to us all. I had gone to Middlesborough, and although I had caught the last train from Middlesborough to Darlington, which had arrived at its destination on time, hoping to catch the 02.52 ex-London train to Edinburgh Waverly, the connection from Edinburgh Waverly to Inverkeithing, allowing me to arrive back on board on time.

This night it was not to be. There was no sign of the train at 02.52, nor at 03.52, and enquiries only seemed to confuse the issue. All we knew was that heavy air raids had been going on all that night and the services were badly disrupted. I had seen the flashes of guns and bombs from the Darlington train but they had seemed far off.

Eventually, at about 06.05, the train crawled slowly into the station. Over three hours late, now what would happen? Never fear, there were most of the leave takers on that train, and most of them had joined it in London. It now became a case of hope for the best.

The arrival on board of all the mob at once, and all with the same excuse for being adrift over leave, helped matters. Our 1st Lt. had obviously made enquiries and had our excuse confirmed as true, so when he cleared lower deck and had his chat to us all, he then threw down the challenge. If anyone adrift over leave gave him an excuse he had never heard before, then he would let that man off. Several tried, but failed, he did know all the excuses.

In July "BEDOUIN" went in for a refit at Immingham Docks, and we had a couple of weeks leave, and very welcome that was too. To get to Grimsby, we had to catch the electric tram to Grimsby from Immingham docks, quite a fast trip, and a good service too.

It was after leave here that the 1st Lt. met his match. Our very good friend and messmate, Lofty Grattan came off adrift. When the 1st Lt.'s Requestmen and Defaulters was held, there was Lofty in the line, not in the least worried. When he came down to the mess, the question fired at him was, "Well, what did you get, one and one?". "No" he replied, "I got let off". "Bloody hell! How?". "Well", says Lofty, "I told him that I was on the station on time, in fact well before time and the train was due, but then as the train came in, and I was about to board it, a poor old lady who had been waiting fainted. Well, I couldn't just get on the train and leave her lying on the platform, could I? So I went over to give her some assistance, and the train pulled out, leaving me behind. So I couldn't help being late sir, could I?". 1st Lt. "Grattan, you are a first class liar, but I have never heard that one before. Case dismissed".

Soon after leaving the docks and returning to Scapa, Commander J.A. McCoy, became Captain J.A. McCoy D.S.O. This meant that he would be leaving the ship and a new Captain appointed. On the day he left the ship at Scapa, the whole ship's company lined the rails and gave him three hearty cheers, and still cheered him as the boat left the ship. There were tears running from his eyes as he left, for he was well liked and respected, and we showed him that on his departure.

Of the new Captain, we could not quite make him out at first. Commander Brian G. Scurfield looked at first to be a strictly Pusser man. In the first few weeks under his command, we gathered the impression of a man who went strictly by the book. No wearing of the cap flat aback, ie. on the back of the head, night clothing for evening rounds and the such like. He had even been seen on the bridge reading 'The Life of Nelson', a historical biography of the great man's life and battles.

On the other hand, he was very keen to see that we all knew exactly what to do in any emergency, and practised action and damage control, reducing the ship to local control of weaponry, damage to engines and boilers etc, finishing with the steering being done from the tiller flat. Her certainly got the whole ship's company on their toes. In the end, we seemed to be able to do anything in any situation automatically, literally without thinking.

As the year progressed toward winter, and all that winter held in store for us, we were occupied in sweeps along the Norwegian coast looking for stray shipping to sink, or if possible, a stray warship or two to attack.

To go back several months, before the Immingham refit. A most peculiar, indeed mysterious would be more appropriate, happening took place while the ship was at Scapa. At a very early hour on this particular morning, we were awakened and told to dress and not leave the mess. Completely in the dark as to what it was all about, we complied, rather grumpily as one can imaging, the time being before 05.00. The next thing, down came the Gunner (T) accompanied by the 1st Lt. whereupon we were told to open our kit lockers and stand by them as they were searched. Well, we thought, something serious must have happened to warrant this sort of caper. Having been cleared by the search and some questions, such as the old favourite, "Where were you on the night of ...?" etc, etc. We were allowed to relax and get a brew of tea going, and then got washed and shaved.

It transpired that on the previous day, the Paybob and Scribes had drawn the Ship's Company's pay from the appropriate authorities, and had sorted the lot into pay packets for the following day - Pay Day. The tray of packets had then been placed in the Ship's Office safe which, as the Ship's Office was, in reality, only the size of a small cabin, was fixed securely to the stanchion outside the office door.

That night, the Wardroom had a film show, and after the show ended, the Paybob tottered off to the Ship's Office for something he had probably forgotten, and for some reason decided to take a look in the safe and check the pay packets. Much to his amazement, the safe was empty. No pay packets, no tray they had been in, and no sign of any tampering with the safe.

Hence all the searching and questioning. Another emergency drawing of our pay had to be made, and although a little late, we did get it that day. For some weeks after, one would bump into an officer still prowling around looking for the missing tray of pay. Nothing was ever found of that lot of pay, although whoever did the job would have been several hundreds of pounds better off. No tray was ever found, and there were no signs that any pay envelopes had been torn up and thrown over the side. The whole lot had been spirited away without a trace. Moreover, no culprit was found or a suspicion of a culprit. The perfect robbery.

The escorting of the Fleet Carrier H.M.S. "INDOMITABLE" from Scapa became another battle against the elements, and showed how cruel the sea can be. "INDOMITABLE", escorted by four destroyers and the 8" gun cruiser "LONDON", which had recently returned to duty from a complete overhaul, had been rebuilt so that she resembled one of the K.G.V. class battleships, left Scapa at 08.00. The weather, a westerly gale increasing to storm force. Clearing the Pentlands, the force of ships met the rollers coming in from the Atlantic. We, in destroyers, took it as one of the normal run of things, but what of the "INDOMITABLE"?

She had loaded on the full war complement of planes at Scapa, and they were all stowed in the hangars below the flight deck. Now we were meeting the big seas. "INDOMITABLE" began sticking her nose into them. The result of this, heavy pitching combined with rolling. As she dug her bows into the rollers, so great walls of water were heaping on to the flight deck, and with the rise of her bows, the water surged along her flight deck in a foaming wall, pouring over the stern.

This continual heaving, pitching and rolling, combined with the sharp drops as the seas passed under her, had caused the lashings of the planes to strain and break, and the further west we went toward Cape Wrath, the more planes became damaged through breaking loose and crashing into bulkheads and other parked planes.

Cape Wrath was eventually reached at 14.00, but by then "INDOMITABLE" had hardly a flyable plane left, the rest were write-offs, so it was decided to return to Scapa and await a better day. The return, with the wind and sea blowing on our stern, took half the time of the outward journey, but there was plenty of cleaning up to do in the destroyers when we got in.

There came the occasion when the Free French Navy let themselves down badly, and my personal opinion of them took a nose-dive. "BEDOUIN" had been out on one of those '32° west' jobs, and was proceeding back to Scapa alone. Weather conditions had caused a greater than usual call on the fuel oil, and thus her furnace fuel oil tanks were in a very low state, and we were steaming at the best economical speed in order to preserve our fuel.

From out of the blue came a signal. As "BEDOUIN" was the nearest and the most available ship, we were to proceed to a position 180 miles from the Butt of Lewis, westerly, where a merchant ship had been torpedoed by a U-Boat. We had to make all speed possible, and then carry out a 24 hour square search. This was later altered to a 48 hour search.

A hurried consultation was held between the Captain and the Engineer Officer. We could steam at 30 knots for the six hours it required to get to the scene of the reported sinking, and then carry out the search at about 6 knots, this leaving us a bare necessity of fuel to reach Scapa, provided weather held good.

So turning round and flashing up the third boiler, which was always kept banked at sea, speed increased to 30 knots. A long swell was running from the Atlantic, and the order was given to clear the upper deck. The reason became all too obvious as the ship began crashing its way through the rollers. The spray from the bows dipping into the swell was hurtling inboard with the force of grapeshot, a seething white wall of spray. We were hitting milestones with monotonous regularity, the bows crashing down into the oncoming swell and throwing the sea and spray high, wide and handsome. A most uncomfortable six hours.

It now became known why we had been told off for this job when we were so low on fuel. A Free French destroyer had been detailed for this job, but the crew had, in as many words, mutinied. They refused to put to sea alone because they said it was too dangerous for one ship to be out there alone. What, in Heavens name, did they think we were, a whole flotilla? My trust in the ability and the sincerity of the French Navy went down to rock bottom, and I imagine the rest of the crew of "BEDOUIN" must have felt similarly.

Nothing was found during the search, not even any evidence that a ship had been sunk in the area, so after the 48 hours were up, we limped off home. By keeping to a very economical speed, we made the north of Scottish coast at Cape Wrath and made our slow way back to Scapa. Now our troubles started all over again. A sudden drop in speed, white smoke pouring from the funnels, and the Captain demanding to know what was happening in the engine and boiler rooms. It turned out to be that we were so low on fuel that the bilge water that invariably collect in the fuel tanks was being fed into the furnace along with the fuel oil, thus causing the white smoke and the loss of heating in the boilers.

We made Scapa with barely enough fuel oil to get us to the tanker. We were far below the allowed minimum before refuelling, the 25% minimum had been well broken. Fortunately, no damage had been done to the boilers or the firebricks in the furnace area by the injection of water with the fuel.

On one sweep along the Norwegian coast, the A/S made a contact, which at the first instant, seemed to be a submarine contact, except that this one did not appear to be doing what a submarine would do when it had been detected. This was puzzling, to say the least, yet the contact still came slowly toward us.

It was probably a good thing that the night was clear and starlit, with a sliver of a moon giving just a little light. The sea was calm, and as we moved slowly through the water, not showing any bow wave or stern wash, somebody forward of the bridge suddenly shouted urgently "Mine on port bow". That brought the sightseers on to the upper deck. There was the perishing thing heading straight for us, bobbing around in the gentle waves.

There seemed to be no way of avoiding the mine, but with the engines stopped and the rudder hard over to port, the mine now tended to float close by on the port side. To be on the safe side, the Captain ordered bearing off spars to be brought into action, taking care not to touch or damage the horns of the mine. We did not know, and could not tell, whether it was German or British.

The delicate game of touch and push went the whole length of the ship until finally the mine drifted clear of the stern, when a touch ahead on the engines sent it still further from us. Only then did we let our breath out fully as we all sighed with relief.

In November 1941 came the turn of "BEDOUIN" to take part in a Russian convoy. First we sailed to our favourite refuelling service in Iceland, Seydis Fiord, to top up before taking over the convoy north of Iceland from the American escort.

It appeared that at this period of time, the Germans had not realised what was going on behind their backs, and our real worry was U-Boats, if any were able to operate in this area. However, at this time of the year, our progress would be pretty well screened by the long hours of darkness. It was so with this convoy.

The weather helped inasmuch that it remained fairly good, so the convoy was able to progress at a fair speed. The usual precautions were taken aboard all H.M. ships with the anti-icing and operation of all weapons every fifteen minutes. This alone kept us all wide awake and watchful.

The uneventful outward passage ended in the Kola Inlet, where the convoy parted company with the escort and sailed on into

Murmansk. H.M. ships all refuelled off a Russian tanker, and some of us took the chance to hop over and see how the other half lived. After anchoring, and during a free period, I thought it a good idea to nip up on to the bridge and find out what the temperature was. The sun shone as if it were a mid-summers day in Britain so, clad only in overall trousers and singlet, I went up to the bridge, not feeling the least cold, but when I read the thermometer, I had second thoughts. It showed 24° of frost (8°F or -13.5°C).

That same night, a couple of Russian destroyers joined the British escort for a raid and bombardment on Petsamo, an island off the most northerly coast of Norway. A fast dash along the coast, and then the bombardment, for Petsamo had been taken over by the Germans and they were using it as an air base.

The most annoying thing about the raid lay in the Russian destroyers getting themselves into such a position that they blocked out our guns, we could not fire for fear of hitting them. Again, we were using flashless cordite, which helped us to hide our positions, but not so with the Russians, they were using cordite which made a flash bright enough to illuminate half of Moscow. Again, I suppose it was our good fortune that the enemy were either caught unawares or had nothing handy to oppose us with.

Back at the Kola Inlet, we picked up the empty convoy returning to the States, and set forth on the return journey. On the way towards Bear Island, the weather blew up and I well remember on my 21st birthday, off Bear Island, being at Captain's Requestmen, being granted my first Good Conduct Badge in the Plot, with the Captain and I facing each other and as the ship pitched and rolled, swaying toward and then away from each other. Oh Happy 21st Birthday!

At the start of that Russian convoy, we had been allowed to discontinue shaving, and those who wished to carry on growing a beard would have to request to continue not shaving. The Captain would judge whether he thought a man's whiskers were suitable enough or not. Many and varied were the beards when we reached Scapa, but sadly for many, only a very few were good enough for the Owner. So many once familiar faces began once more to emerge from out of the straggly undergrowth that had grown during the Russian trip.

Our arrival back at Scapa actually meant a few days in harbour this time, but something else had been put in the pipeline for us, an operation which was meant to be a diversionary raid for another operation in the south of Norway at a place called Vaagso. The Vaagso raid actually took place on Christmas Day 1941 and created havoc among the Germans. The choice of Christmas Day simply meant 'Do to them as they would do to you, only do it first'.

The diversionary force were to make their appearance on Boxing Day, and to remain in the area as long as possible. The force consisted of two cruisers, four destroyers, a tanker and supply ship. The orders were to make a base in some remote fiord, and create as much havoc as possible.

The weather, which had turned foul, helped to screen our movements approaching our target area, the Lofoten Islands. On Christmas Day, I had the forenoon watch, and on being relieved at 12.30, went down to my mess for dinner. Christmas dinner, roast pork, roast spuds and peas. To try to sit down to eat it was impossible, the ship was doing everything except looping the loop, so the only thing I could do was to wrap one arm and one leg around a stanchion at the foot of the ladder, and try to eat my food that way.

On Boxing Day, the strike force had entered the Vest Fiord, and found a safe and hidden haven, entering it under the cover of a snow squall. The walls of the high mountains were almost sheer for as high as could be seen, and from where they entered the water, straight down. The ship was able to go within a foot or so of the rock face without any danger of causing any damage to the ship.

The destroyers took it in turns to go out on the rampage in pairs. Now we played the enemy at their own game. As soon as we had cleared the entrance of the hide-out, so under the cover of the first snow shower that came along, and they were very frequent, down came the White Ensign and up went the Swastika. This made the Tribal class destroyers almost indistinguishable from a well known class of German destroyers.

In this way, during the week to ten days we were there, between the destroyers a number of German patrol craft went missing, and nobody on the side of the enemy seemed to twig on to what was going on. Luck cannot last for ever, and at long last Jerry smelled something awfully nasty, so he sent a bomber to find out what. The bomber found our hidey hole, and managed to drop just one bomb, which missed the target, and then visibility beat him.

The Senior Officer aboard the cruisers gave the order to leave, and once again, under the cover of snow showers the whole force slipped out of the Vest Fiord, and sailed to the west our of harms way, and back home to base at Scapa.

Another danger had loomed up on the horizon in the shape of the sister ship to the "BISMARK", the "TIRPITZ". She had slipped out of the Baltic and was even now making her way up the coast of Norway, port by port. She was now believed to be in Bergen, and somehow she had to be stopped from making her way to the northern part of Norway, and becoming a menace to the Russian convoys.

Intelligence reports indicated that the "TIRPITZ" might well be planning to move from Bergen in the near future, so a hasty plan became cobbled together in case the word came that "TIRPITZ" was on the move.

The plan was that eight destroyers should cross to the Norwegian coast at high speed and then carry out a sweep up the coast, keeping speed at 14 knots, the highest speed at which the bow wave would not break and show a white wash. If the "TIRPITZ" showed up, the destroyers were to attack with torpedoes, with the four subdivisions attacking from the four points of the compass. This type of attack ensured that whatever manoeuvre the "TIRPITZ" made, she was sure to be hit by one or more torpedoes, and possibly badly damaged, hopefully enough to put her out of circulation for a while. If not, any shipping found was to be attacked and sunk.

Word did come that "TIRPITZ" was ready to sail from Bergen, so the destroyer force, which included "BEDOUIN" as Second in Command, sailed from Scapa, steaming at 30 knots in two lines ahead one nautical mile apart. On the way across, "PUNJABI", steaming astern of "BEDOUIN", complained of steering problems, and had eventually to leave the line and return to Scapa. On sped the remaining seven destroyers. Then close, dangerously close, to the Norwegian coast and south of Bergen, speed came down to 14 knots and the sweep formation assumed.

All ships were at all night action stations, and there were probably more pairs of eyes peering into the blackness of that night, than there had ever been before. Each and every person on deck that night had their eyes peeled for trouble in the shape of Germany's latest battleship. In the event, nothing was seen of "TIRPITZ", and nothing was seen of any other shipping either, and if there were any, they had probably taken the inshore channels.

So before first light in the morning, the seven destroyers turned for home and arrived in Scapa with nothing more than a sleepless night to show for our trouble. It later turned out that "TIRPITZ" had, in fact, left Bergen the night before our sweep and gone south.

At this point I must transgress and go back some months. A certain young Able Seaman (Trained Man) had made a request to transfer to the Submarine Service, but before he left the ship he wanted to train as a Torpedoman, and thus came into the Torpedomen's mess. Peter soon became known as 'Periscope Pete', and his ideas of submarines and submarine warfare must have come straight out of Naval fiction or too many Yank films.

A good lad in many respects, he did have the inclination to be a bit heavy handed. This became borne out when, after servicing a torpedo, he was asked to disconnect the air line from the air valve. Having disconnected the air line at both ends, he then grabbed hold of a spanner and attacked the air valve. It was still hissing some air so, instead of turning the valve off properly by means of the handwheel on the top of the valve, he used a large spanner. Oh yes, he turned the valve off alright, and in doing so, managed to wrench the whole valve clean off level with the deck.

Although the valve was replaced within a couple of days, a very displeased C.E.R.A. had surveyed the damage muttering something to the effect of "Who let your pet monkey out of his cage?". In any case, a valve such as that type, will let out air, because once it is disconnected from whatever it is supplying, it will release the pressure in the pipe.

This event preceded another mishap, which I think is permissable to tell about, as it happened some 53 years ago. We were to run a single tiddler, using a blowing head. So the requisite fish was prepped, the warhead removed, and the blowing head fitted on. The blowing head was now filled with water, and the air hose inserted into the air bottle valve. In the engine room, the E.R.A. was standing by the compressor to start it up as soon as we had connected up.

Everything ready, and the signal given to the E.R.A. to start compressor. As usual we wandered off for a quick burn while the pressure built up in the blowing head air bottle, which normally took about five minutes. Not this day though. Pressure was up in half the normal time, but nobody really thought about that as being not quite right. So, tiddler prepped, blowing head ready, close down until firing in the morning.

The following morning, out into the Flow steamed "BEDOUIN", and fires one fish. Then turning on to the course taken by our minnow, we followed track, at a much lower speed of course, and reaching the point where there should have been one in number, torpedo, complete with blowing head emitting smoke, we found to our great surprise that our lovely little fish had vanished, the question was, where to? and why?

After much searching, it finally sunk in that one £3,000 torpedo had got itself lost. Then came the enquiries, questions did we do this? Yes. Did we do that? Yes. There was talk of sending divers down to try and find it, but we had fired it in the close proximity of the wreck of the "ROYAL OAK", so that idea died a natural death. In the end, the whole thing was treated as an unsolvable mystery.

Weeks later, when the whole affair of the missing fish had been forgotten, the E.R.A. concerned who had run up the compressor, came over to the tubes, where the tubes crew were carrying out another routine, and quietly said "I've been having thoughts on that missing fish. Can you tell me which compressor you were connected up to?". "Yes", came the reply. "The starboard one. Why?". "Well, keep it under you hat, I ran up the port compressor, and wondered why it reached 2000 so quickly." "Oh no. You keep quiet as well, and let's hope that fish is never found." Thereafter, any time we used the compressors, we made absolutely certain that the Tiffy knew which one we were connected to.

When Winston Churchill went to the U.S.A. in December 1941 to see President Roosevelt on a mission to hammer out the details of some agreement, he was taken there aboard the battleship "DUKE OF YORK". "BEDOUIN" formed part of the escort of four destroyers which took them to the position where the destroyers left the "DUKE OF YORK" to continue to America on her own at high speed, 32° west. Still steaming in line abreast, the destroyers, steaming at 20 knots, made their way toward Scapa, heading into an ever increasing wind and sea. An easterly gale blew up, and gradually increased into a storm force 10.

"BEDOUIN" had on her starboard side Captain (D), and with the sea and wind getting ever stronger, the four ships were having difficulty making headway. The Butt of Lewis had been seen and apparently passed. Speed had been reduced to 12 knots by this time, and fuel was getting a bit low. Then two things happened. Captain (D) signalled for "BEDOUIN" to take over as he had gone sick. The next was somebody asking what was that light over there, pointing to starboard.

That light should have been Cape Wrath, but it was slowly moving ahead of us. That light was found to be the Butt of Lewis, and we were being blown astern at 3 knots. In those conditions there was only on thing to do, find shelter. Speed was increased enough to make headway, and the small force of destroyers managed to get into the Minches, and getting as close to the weather shore as possible for shelter, then went into line ahead, and cracked on speed to 25 knots.

The sea in the Minches had been blown flat by the wind, and this was the first time that I had ever been aboard a ship doing 25 knots and being blown into a list of 10° to starboard by the wind. Our destination was Loch Alsh, and there we all found shelter and could refuel. We might have been out of the wind, but certainly not out of the rain, it poured down. Our re-entry into Scapa was about 48 hours late.

Although the U.S.A. did not officially enter the war until 7th December 1941, after Pearl Harbour, they did have a force present in the European sphere. The battleship "WASHINGTON" and the aircraft carrier "WASP", along with a number of destroyers had arrived in Scapa Flow, and during the fine weather months, carried out a number of exercises with the Home Fleet, where the Yank destroyers screened the Home Fleet battleships and carriers, and we British destroyers did likewise to the Yank big ships.

I well remember one fine day when "BEDOUIN" and two other destroyers were detailed off to screen the carrier "WASP". As we were leaving the Flow, the "WASP" signalled across to us, 'Can you raise steam for 45 knots?'. The Captain, quick as a flash, replied 'Yes, and more if required'. That must have shut loudmouth up, for we never exceeded over 20 knots all day.

The "WASHINGTON" and the "NELSON" went out at the same time to do a full calibre 16" gun shoot at a battle practice target, and were positioned well to the north of "WASP" and her attendant destroyers, but that did not prevent the "WASHINGTON" from firing one shot in our direction, although it sailed well over our heads, splashing down clear of the group.

Then a flying boat from the "WASP" took a nosedive into the sea, and became a piece of floating wreckage. We rescued the crew, and the Captain decided to try to salvage the plane. After several abortive attempts to take it in tow, and the breaking of a number of steel wire hawsers, the crew of the plane went up to the bridge. The conversation went something like this: "Hey, Cap'n, don't bother with that load of old junk. Jest cut it free and sink the goddam thing." A frosty look from the Captain, but he cut the plane adrift, and then turned around and steamed at it, ramming right through the fuselage, and ensuring that the wreck would then sink.

Now that the Hun had discovered our crafty plot to supply Russians with arms and other supplies by convoys to the northern Russian ports, activity started on the northern coast of Norway. The fear that Germany might well send surface craft to the northern Norwegian ports to dart out and interfere with the convoys, kept a large fleet either at Scapa on full alert or in Iceland, from where they could reach the North Cape of Norway or the Bear Island area fairly quickly, but this idea soon turned into patrols off the North Cape of Norway, and to the south of any of the passing convoys, either outward or inward.

On one of those triangular patrols, the force left Scapa in reasonable weather not more than a force 8 gale blowing. Four destroyers, which included "BEDOUIN", were detached to proceed to Seydis Fiord to refuel and rendezvous with the rest of the Fleet on completion of refuelling.

Shortly after leaving Seydis Fiord, the weather began to get a bit heavy, but not enough to be any worry. By the time I went on watch at 08.00 for the forenoon watch, the depth charges had been pushed out of the trap on the stern, and were rolling about the Quarterdeck. They were duly caught and lashed securely. I could now see that mountainous waves were coming at the ship, and as the waves passed under us, we were brought to the top of the wave, but no other destroyer could be seen unless, that is, another ship rode to the top of a wave at the same time.

The big ships could be seen fractionally before we slipped down into the trough of the next wave. When visible, it could be seen that the "VICTORIOUS" was shipping seas right over her flight deck, and the two battleships were digging in their noses, while the "LONDON" seemed to be riding the lot with ease.

Then, about noon, came the order to alter course 135° to port. This would now put the sea on the starboard quarter. This alteration, of course, took 75 minutes to execute, simply because every time the bows started to move to port, a wave would knock the ship back to the original course again. When the bows really started to move round to port, everything became easier. The shuddering ceased, and although the position of the sea on the quarter made the ship roll more, the motion had become more comfortable.

The seas gradually abated and it became much easier to carry out course changes, and other evolutions concerned with station keeping and deployment of destroyers. Unfortunately another hazard cropped up, ice. We had now reached the time to return to Scapa.

Snow and rain squalls, combined with blown spray, had gradually settled on the superstructure and funnels, and unnoticed had started to form a layer of ice. Such were the temperatures in these northern climes at mid-winter. Despite efforts to eliminate the threat, the ice steadily grew and the closer to Scapa we got, the thicker the ice grew. The feeling of top-heaviness in the ship began to be felt, and we were glad when the Orkneys hove in sight.

The Engineer Officer estimated that there were about 200 tons of ice in all, and we entered Scapa Flow with all available hands chipping ice off the superstructure. I would not guess at the thickness of the ice on the superstructure, but fire axes were being used to chip it away. I would estimate about six inches on the funnels. Nobody wanted that experience again.

The whole Fleet had gone to Iceland in February 1942, and were anchored in Hval Fiord. The destroyers were doing duty guardships, and taking turns at patrolling outside the fiord from the Denmark Strait to the Grenadiers, a small line of islands about 12 miles off the Icelandic south-east coast, and south of Reykjavik. The Fleet lay there awaiting intelligence of the movements of any German ship, from E-Boats to battleships. That intelligence was not long in coming in.

On 12th February 1942, the "SCHARNHORST", "GNEISEN-AU" and "PRINZ EUGEN" had slipped out of Brest, and accompanied by destroyers and E-Boats, had steamed up the Channel. The Home Fleet, alerted at last could only make a high speed dash to try to stop them getting too far north. It was a vain attempt, for they had all put into either Baltic ports or southern Norwegian ports, where they would be safely under the umbrella of the Luftewaffe.

All ships returned to Scapa, (even there would have been too far from the enemy ships to stop them getting to Baltic ports) and awaited for another chance on another day. In the meantime, the Bear Island/North Cape patrols must still go on.

Once again the familiar force of battleships, carrier, cruisers and destroyers left Scapa. This time things were to work out slightly different. The weather was foul for a start. Wind approaching hurricane force, and visibility poor. Only one gate would be opened to let out the fleet, and that was the main exit from the Flow, or the big ships gateway.

Passing through the gate, the full force of the wind hit. The passage through the Pentlands had been expected to be rough, but it was just the opposite. The sea was flat, but the howling wind had heeled the destroyers over to port and the actual surface of the sea could not be seen. We were steaming through a sea of spray, whipped up by the wind to form a fog-like haze, commonly known as sea smoke.

Coming clear of the Pentlands, and turning to the north, the full savagery of the storm hit. Although lifelines were rigged, it had become very chancy trying to get from forrard to aft and vice versa. We had left Scapa in the morning and by late afternoon, signals were coming in from the destroyers on the screen, of men being lost overboard. I was on the bridge, doing my turn there during the watch, and looking aft I could see the seas crashing in over the tubes and all along the iron deck. Looking forward, I could also see the bows disappearing into the heavy waves and throwing water and spray right over the bridge at times.

Somebody had noticed that one of the Carley Rafts on the raft rack aft (a girder structure which stretched from the level of 'X' gun deck to the guard rail position on the iron deck in the form of a bridge with a sloping roof) had become loose through the seas breaking over and under it with such force every few minutes. The 1st Lt. called for the P.O. of the watch and asked for some hands to go aft and secure the Carley Raft, but not to take risks.

Five volunteers made their way aft, and started to relash the raft into position. I had been watching from my perch on the bridge, when suddenly the ship lurched to port, then came upright and without warning heeled over to port again, this time heeling over to 44°. This I know as at that moment I had taken a look at the roll indicator, a curved spirit level on the after binnacle.

Turning to look aft, I saw that the ship had rolled right into an oncoming sea, which had boiled up over the upper deck, reaching as high as the top of the after superstructure. Then in the white wash astern I spotted two black dots. Realising those two dots were men, I carried out the alarm routine without thinking, yelling "Man overboard" and pressing the lifebuoy alarm.

Of the five that had gone to lash the raft down again, three were still with us. One was clinging to the raft, another hanging on to a vertical ladder which gave access to 'X' gun deck, and the third had become entwined in the guard rails, and was hanging on for grim life. A very rapid rescue act, and the three were safe again. But the two who had gone over the side, although the Captain turned the ship and tried to make a search, it was all in vain.

The sea that had done the damage, had also damaged the port turbo-generator, thus cutting our electrical supplies in half, although the diesel generator was brought into service, it had not the same output as the steam generator. Thus we were allowed to make our search for our men, and try to catch up with the rest later. There was a snag to this, as we would not be able to contact them to find their position. Doing so could well endanger the whole force.

Although attempting to follow the other ships, we found ourselves off the Norwegian coast. The weather had moderated somewhat, but the sky was still dark and overcast, with heavy black clouds shutting out any sun.

At about 15.00, an aircraft dropped from out of the clouds astern of us. Flying at a fairly low level, we recognised the plane as a Fokker-Wolfe Condor, a long range spy plane, and it had espied "BEDOUIN" all alone. But no! Had the crew realised who we were? Or were they at that very moment sending off a request for dozens of dive-bombers. Apparently not, they dropped recognition flares. We gave them ours, a burst from our pom-poms. Now that these weapons had been rigged out with self destruct and tracer shells, our gunners could take a rough aim and then hose pipe shoot.

Watching from a good vantage point, I saw a number of those tracer shells hit the plane along the fuselage and better still, right in the control cabin, so perhaps the pilot or others of the crew may well have copped a packet. The plane did jerk and sheer away.

Seconds later our twin 4" guns took part in adding to the discomfort of the aircraft's crew, helping their hurried departure from our proximity. Out of range of our guns, they circled for a time, probably plotting our course and speed, and then as dusk fell, disappeared into the distance.

When the enemy aircraft had left the area, our course and speed were altered so that should any searchers come out looking for us in the early morning light, they would draw a blank. Within a short time we had received our orders to return to base, and we entered Scapa from the west a couple of days later.

With the threat of the three German battleships at large, plus the heavy cruiser "PRINZ EUGEN" and others of that ilk not so very far away, the whole Fleet based at Scapa were constantly at sea.

On one excursion into enemy water, the weather was so bad that we destroyers were pitching so heavily that we were hitting 'milestones' every few minutes. "BEDOUIN" hit one such 'milestone' one night during the middle watch, about 01.30. The ship dropped back so heavily after climbing over a high wave, that the shock of hitting the water made everything in the mess shelf rise and fall out on to the deck, except that which fell into old Sam Sayer's hammock, which was slung directly below the shelf.

Cups, saucers, plates, tinned food, Pussers dried marrowfat peas, just everything came crashing down. Perhaps, by a stroke of good fortune, only a few pieces of our crockery got broken, probably the fall being broken by Sam's hammock. The noise made by the falling tins, however, woke up nearly all the sleeping occupants of our mess, and a scramble began to pick up the pieces and articles that had shot out of the mess shelf.

One of the side effects of this was that while preparing the dinner a few days later, it was decided to clear out the odds and ends left in the mess shelf, and around the mess for that matter. When we asked what was for afters, the answer came back, figgy duff. That did it. Sam and myself went through everything we could find which would cook, or could be put into a duff. Apart from the normal ingredients of flour, fat, sugar, and raising powder, the extras included desiccated coconut, Epsom salts, Eno's fruit salts, to name a few. The result when it came down into the mess that dinner time, turned out to be the best steamed duff for months.

Somebody (obviously in a high place) thought it a good idea if the Carrier "VICTORIOUS" could get close in to the Norwegian coast, fly off a heap of her 'Stringbags', fully loaded with bombs and take a look up some of the fiords and see if there were any stray targets about to sink or blow up. As per expected, "BEDOUIN" and two other destroyers were given their 'Take up the screen' orders, so off we toddled to Norway again.

With the Norwegian coast only about 200 miles off, we in "BEDOUIN", got a nice loud 'ping'. Classified as submarine, we prepared to attack, set the staggered depths on the charges, and waited for the moment to drop them. Then came a garbled message, and poor old Lofty Grattan operating the trap, got the message as only three charges. The came the attack, and off went the throwers and one from the trap. Then, Lofty, straining with all his might, managed to stop the two remaining charges being dropped from the trap.

The nett result from this was the Captain wanting to know what the hell was going on down aft, and why only three charges, where were the other two. As this antic was being sorted out, the Ping Bo'sun had declared the contact had not, after all, been a submarine contact at all so, reloading the trap and the throwers, we all returned to normal.

When the time came for "VICTORIOUS" to fly off her aircraft, we all had to turn into the wind and increase speed. The planes used were the later 'Stringbags', slightly faster and with a covered cockpit, and were known as 'Albacores'.

We waved them off and wished them luck as they formed up into flights and droned off toward an unknown fate. One thing we could absolutely bank on, that they would most certainly be given a violently hostile reception. The drill in this case was, fly to target, plaster it well, then get out at best speed and return to Scapa. This last meant that they would not be landing on again after the raid, that would be asking for trouble, and possibly the loss of the carrier.

As soon as the last plane had taken off, "VICTORIOUS" gave the order to turn away from Norway, and speed increased again. Some hours later there came the drone of British aero engines, and the first of the attack force passed overhead, waving like mad. Some of them looked a bit seedy, with bits of cloth fuselage waving in the breeze, holes in the wings, and tailplanes and rudder. But it was well known that the Albacore, like the Swordfish, could fly on the ribs of their wings. "VICTORIOUS" and the three destroyers then altered course to get as far as possible away from Norway, before making for Scapa.

About the end of March, after one long and gruelling trip, we entered Scapa to find that the Yanks were there. "BEDOUIN" had to go alongside the Depot ship for some rather obscure reason, and parked alongside on the other side of the Depot ship were a couple of Yank destroyers.

Being friendly people, one or two of us thought it a good idea to go over and make our pennants known. So saying, off we went, and stepping aboard the nearest ship, got into conversation with members of the crew. They certainly had a long tale of woe, for we heard that it had taken them ten whole days to cross from Bermuda to Scapa, and they had bad weather all the way, well bad to them, because they had been stuck with a monotonous roll all the way over.

Our thoughts on that problem of the Yanks made us refrain from asking if they had ever been round Bear Island when the wind blows. Instead we opted for a guided tour of the ship, a 'Benson' class destroyer. Taken down below, we soon saw the difference between the Yanks and our ships. We slept in hammocks, most comfortable at sea, while they all had bunks. Our messes were where we ate, slept, and took our few pleasures, like card games or 'Uckers'. The Yanks had a dining hall and recreation space.

In the engine room and at the switchboards, and in almost every compartment there were coffee makers and Pepsi machines, and ice-cream literally on tap. This last, of course, gave rise to the British Naval song, sang to the Yank Marine Corps Prayer, which went thus:

> "From the halls of Montezuma to the shores of Italy,
> There's a buzz going round the harbour that the Yanks are going to sea,
> With a bottle of Pepsi Cola and a f****** great tub of ice-cream,
> For they're bloody good kids in harbour, but oh my gawd at sea!"

That song, of course, came after the landings in North Africa, but was very popular still long after the war ended.

It has been said, in the best of circles, that the Yanks, when they build a ship, fit the crew in first, and then find room for the armament, engines and magazines etc., but the British first fit the ship with all its armament, magazines and engines etc. and then find room for the crew. At that time looking at the Yanks ships, and then at our own, it would seem that the above quote would be correct.

The seemingly unending patrols went on, but no sign of any enemy ships could be seen. Just the same, alertness was still the name of the game. Scapa had become a perfect haven. The entrance by which the U-Boat had reached the Flow and sunk the "ROYAL OAK" had been sealed off, and the German Air Force had learned not to try anything on after their first abortive effort right at the beginning of the war when they lost 75% of the planes they sent over to the fire power of both the Fleet and the Scapa Barrage, which had to be seen to be believed and appreciated.

At long last came the orders we had been long awaiting, proceed for docking. Since losing the two men overboard, there had been a 'Dean Man's Kit' auction. In this, each item of the deceased person is held up for the best bid, and with things like shorts, underpants, vests, the sold item would often be thrown back into the kitty to be reauctioned several times. This was always done to swell the proceeds, all of which went to the next of kin. A sad thought perhaps, but a little hard cash handed over with the man's personal belongings showed that his shipmates were feeling people who had tried to give help as best they could, in the only way they could and knew.

Before leaving Scapa, we torpedomen thought it a good idea to clear our mess of any accumulated rubbish, and clear out underneath the hammock netting. Here I found a little surprise in the shape of a pile of Pussers peas that had been shed when we hit the aforementioned milestone. A trickle of water, probably condensation, had gone under the netting and the peas, or some of them, had rolled into this tiny strip of moisture, and surprisingly had started to shoot. I grabbed them quickly and stowed them all away in a bag to take home.

The journey to Hull, and up the Humber into the Fish Docks, where we were due to be refitted, was completely uneventful. De-ammunitioning took place immediately, and once that was finished, the first leave party, of which I was one, were allowed to clean into shore going rig, ready to start our leave.

Leaving the ship about 17.00, we were all waved through the gate by the Dockyard Police with a "Have a good leave", and were able to catch the 18.00 train from Hull, Paragon Station, to Doncaster. Sam Sayer had been into the fish packing building and had managed to obtain a box of fish which, needless to say, stank out the carriage compartment.

Changing at Doncaster, the train from there arrived in London, Kings Cross at 05.00 next morning, and taxiing across to Charing Cross, I got the early train home, arriving on the doorstep just as my Father and Sister were about to leave for work in London.

Leave, as it always is, sleeping, going out meeting others you know, a drink now and again, and in general, taking it easy. Forget the war, unless it is to put some know-all's nose out of joint. In this respect, one evening I went to the local hop, and sitting down at a table slowly consuming a drink, I was approached by a young lad all dressed up in his number ones, cap tally bearing the inscription H.M.S. There also happened to be a young lady sitting there at that table as well.

The lad sat down, and then started up the conversation, obviously with the intention of making himself sound like an old hand. I sat there listening, with my elbows on the table and my hands round my biceps, thus hiding my G.C. badge and my non-sub rating's badge. Then the boyo started on about sea service, and turning to me, made some remark about it being tough at sea. I just nodded my head, and the lad went on, of course, you haven't been to sea yet, have you? I casually replied to the effect of not if you say so mate, but if you will pipe down for a few minutes, I'll nip off to the heads, and we can carry on the talk later. Then standing up, I picked my cap up off the floor, put it on the table and asked him to look after it till I came back. He saw his mistake, I was a one badge torpedoman, he was a boy trainee at H.M.S. "ST. GEORGE" on the Isle of Man. Squashed flat. Well, you were always meeting them in those days, and always trying to impress someone.

A conversation between my parents and I one evening jogged my mind about a couple of things that had been partially forgotten. Firstly, about an Irish seaman we had aboard "BEDOUIN". He came from Southern Ireland, a lad of placid disposition, but a wee bit slow thinking. At one time, during the first year of the war, the ship had been going alongside an oiler to refuel. Paddy was standing by the guard-rails clutching a heaving line. As the distance closed to a few feet, someone yelled to Paddy to throw the heaving line. He did. All of it. He had totally forgotten to hold on to the end so that he could heave in the securing hawser from the tanker. Grinning seamen on the oiler promptly sent the heaving line back, but attached to the spring it was intended for. Paddy survived the good natured ragging he got after the event.

The second of Paddy's misfortunes came not so very long before the docking order arrived in the ship. This time it was during a night watch. The time came for the masthead lookout to be relived, and it was Paddy's turn to go aloft. He reached the bottom of the Jacob's ladder that went to the crows nest. The ship, with a heavy sea on her starboard bow, rolled some 20° to port, and some 15° to starboard. As Paddy mounted the ladder, the ship gave an extra lurch to port. Paddy clutched the ladder with the fervour of a fanatical witch doctor grabbing his favourite totem pole.

Up in the crows nest, the lookout waiting to be relieved looked down and shouted something, which obviously must have been obnoxious, after all, he had been shut in that tree top perch for the last hour, and it was freezing cold. Admonition from above had no effect on Paddy, he couldn't hear a thing being yelled down at him anyway.

Bit by bit Paddy inched up the ladder, with every roll to port the ladder swung out over the sea, and with the roll back to starboard, it swung in toward the mast. The further up the ladder Paddy got, the slower became his progress. By now fifteen minutes had passed, and Paddy had barely reached halfway up the ladder. Then Paddy stuck. He would neither go upward nor would be come downward. The P.O. of the watch went to try to edge Paddy upwards, but to no avail. He then tried to get Paddy to come down, but again Paddy refused to move.

Up in the crows nest, the lookout waiting to be relieved couldn't believe his bad luck. By this time he was livid with rage at not being relieved on time. The P.O. of the watch finally pacified the lookout, and sent for help to get Paddy down from his precarious position. Not before time, Paddy at long last, with someone at his side and another below him, started the slow, tedious, descent of the ladder.

By this time, the change of lookout was about to take place. The poor old lad who had spent two hours in the crows nest was not at all pleased with Paddy, and quite ready to murder him out of hand. However, in the end he did see the funny side of it, and let Paddy off. Paddy though, when he had come down from the ladder, was shaking like a leaf. The dark and the swaying ladder had put the wind right up him, it scared him from ever going aloft again.

It was a remark by my Mother about the cruiser H.M.S. "EURAYLUS". This ship had been built in Chatham Dockyard, launched in 1940 and commissioned in 1941. Mother showed her interest in "EURAYLUS" because she, as a Wren in Chatham Barracks, had been to the launch of her, and had watched her subsequent departure from Chatham Dockyard for trials and taking up her war station. "BEDOUIN" had been detailed as escort for her when she did her full power trial.

"BEDOUIN" had met "EURAYLUS" down the east coast somewhere in the region of the Tees/Tyne part of the coast. When we met, "EURAYLUS'" speed had reached about 20 knots after the slow crawl through the swept channel along the Thames Estuary to the Wash, in which channel the German aircraft were quite liable to lay a few magnetic or acoustic mines in the hope of catching an unwary ship doing the wrong speed. The restrictions in the swept channel in this area were below 9 knots or above 25 knots. Anything in between would be likely to set off an acoustic mine under the unfortunate ship.

Once on screen, "BEDOUIN" turned and matched her speed with that of "EURAYLUS". Now the speed signals from "EURAYLUS" began, "I am doing 24 knots", and up went the revs on "BEDOUIN". Slowly "EURAYLUS" raised her speed to 30 knots, and then inched up to 34 knots. Now, our Captain thought, and said, let us see if "EURAYLUS" can match our speed. At this time "BEDOUIN" badly needed a boiler clean, but on went the revs and up went the speed to 35 knots and then 36 knots, slowly pulling away from "EURAYLUS", until when she was almost on the horizon, when she signalled "Come back "BEDOUIN". I cannot keep up with you." If my memory serves me right, "EURAYLUS" went on to make a name for herself, and survived the war. Of her ultimate fate I am unaware.

Air raids over the London area were, at this time, very sporadic. Jerry had lost too many aircraft in the south-west of England. Their efforts were being made in areas more to the north. My leave finished, and feeling refreshed after getting in some well earned proper sleep, I returned to the chaos that represented a refit in full swing.

One of the first things organised was a Ship's dance at one of the local halls. The whole idea of this was to get to know the locals well, and provide a night of fun and dancing at a cheap rate, although the proceeds from the jig would be given to the Ship's fund, and sent off to the next of kin to those two lost overboard. This first dance was only a feeler for a bigger do later on, probably a week or less before we sailed again.

Then came the sporadic raids. Our local pub, The Star, opposite the dockyard gate and across the Hessle Road on the corner with a side street, received a bomb in the rear yard just after dark one evening, soon after the first leave party had returned. On board the short range A.A. automatic guns had been manned, although what they may have been able to do is anybodies guess. Nobody was hurt by that bomb, but it was a warning of things to come. After all, the Fish Docks were a legitimate target, ships moored in them.

During working hours, it was the dockyard workmen that caused the most trouble, especially with their wandering leads. Bill Cook and myself nearly got blinded by one of those. A workman down in the boiler room kept complaining that his light kept going out. After repairing a certain fuse several times, for this dockie had tucked the bare ends of his wander lead behind the fuses in the nearest fuse box, and getting rather fed up with it all, we repaired the fuse again, this time banking it up a little. Fatal. Putting the fuse in, it blew again, this time we caught the flash right across our eyes.

Furious with the workman for bringing in a faulty lead, I spotted the fault, it was draped through a steel ladder and hanging down from a steel rung. Where it hung across the rung the wires were completely bare, so without any more ado, we pulled the lead from the fuse box and hurling it across the boiler room deck, we told the workman to get himself another lead and make sure it was good, then come and see us before putting it in any box.

Shortly before the refit ended, I had spent the evening at a dance. On leaving an air raid started. The raid though was at the eastern end of the town, and nothing came over the Hessle area. Lofty Boyce however, had escorted some young wench right into the area where the raid was. When he arrived back on board the next morning, he was in quite a mess, he had, so he said, been helping the A.R.P. Wardens and the rescue workers trying to find any casualties, or people buried under the rubble. He looked as if he had been digging somewhere too.

Eventually the refit came to an end, and the ship re-ammunitioned, re-stored, and refuelled ready to leave dock. Only one other incident remains to be told. The sentry on the gangway was always armed with a loaded rifle. On one particular night, the sentry had been to the Star before going on sentry duty, and took over his post drunk. A lad coming off shore was challenged by the drunken sentry. "Halt! Who goes there?", and then pulled the trigger. Result, one lad coming off shore and getting shot in the chest. He survived, but was left behind in hospital. The sentry landed in the Glass House. And one member of the crew failed to return from leave, he went on the run. And so ended that refit.

CHAPTER TWO

Refit completed. What lies ahead?

May 31st 1942. A normal early summer's day with, as one might well expect, some small fleecy clouds hanging in an otherwise clear sky, and a warm sun shining. H.M.S. "BEDOUIN", refitted for very cold climates, and with the added attraction of Hammer Gear for the blowing up of acoustic mines, slipped from her berth in the Fish Docks at Hull, and into the Humber River.

For the rest of the day she would be carrying out those very important tests and trials which had to be done after every docking. First came the runs overs the de-gaussing range. This was to determine the Ship's 'Signature', ie to ensure that the degaussing gear aboard was doing its job properly. Next the much more elaborate and lengthy trial, Swinging the Compass. This trial entailed many alterations of course, combined with the adding or taking away of magnets from the binnacle of the magnetic compass. This test was to correct for any alterations which may have taken place likely to throw the magnetic compass out of true whilst in dock.

Trials competed, and shore side staff delivered back to their base, it was now dusk and "BEDOUIN" slipped slowly down the Humber toward the open sea. A very low speed was kept in order that enemy aircraft would not spot the ship and decide that it would be a nice place to lay a few eggs, understandable, because there is no room for manoeuvre in the Humber estuary. However, many of us not below decks at the time, heard the unsynchronised moan of the Jerry planes passing above us as they went in to bomb Hull. For the second time we had beat them and sailed before they arrived.

Once out in the open sea, and dawdling northwards, thoughts turned to what was in store for us. The ship had been fitted out for Russian convoy duty and all aboard knew that "BEDOUIN" was top of the roster for another turn. So for the time being it was all conjecture, we had the knowledge of what happened to PQ convoys earlier in the year. We had done an uneventful one in November 1941.

Early on 1st June we were off the Tyne, and started that very important test Full Power Trial, in which we tried to reach our maximum speed conducive to power output and fuel consumption. The trial lasted from the Tyne to Scapa Flow, where we refuelled and went to our berth at Lyness. Mail received and distributed, letter writing commenced and so ended that day.

The next morning, 2nd June, the usual Daily Routine being carried out when on the Destroyer Depot Ship carrying Rear Admiral Destroyers, a long string of pennant numbers was hoisted to the upper yard. Prominent among them was G67. It was Captain's of those ships shown to go to a conference with RA(D).

Once again the ship came alive with all sorts of buzzes and bright ideas, mostly about which Russian convoy we were about to sail with. However, nothing was given away by the Captain or any of the Wardroom, probably due to their knowing nothing as well.

However, orders were given to be prepared to slip the following morning and we sailed about 08.30 on 3rd June, bound for the Clyde. It took the full 24 hours to reach Greenock, where we anchored off Tail o' Bank. No shore leave was granted, although a last mail drop ashore was made, usual in these circumstances. One could not help noticing however, that some merchant ships were there when we arrived, and by dusk all had disappeared. Then as darkness fell, we weighed anchor and proceeded to sea.

The following morning, 5th June, steaming on a westerly course, there were the disappearing merchantmen of the day before. We were part of their escort, but to where? All we knew was that we had the cruiser H.M.S. "KENYA" in charge carrying the flag of a Vice Admiral. So what did that mean?

Where we were heading for soon became known. It was now 6th June, and the Captain's Steward appeared from nowhere to inform all and sundry about him that the Captain had asked Navvy (the Navigating Officer, otherwise known as 'Pilot') for charts of the areas around Lagos and Freetown, West Africa. Convoys were often taken to and from those two ports about this time, so why should we not be taking one there as well.

The sea remained calm, with the normal long swell usual in the North Atlantic, a submarine's periscope could be seen from several miles off, if a U-Boat Commander had been unwise enough to raise one. Although several contacts were made by other ships, and some attacks carried out, all were deemed to be non-submarine.

Then came the contact made by "BEDOUIN". A certain submarine contact, moving about the speed of a submerged U-Boat, and making slow alterations of course as might be expected. Having become certain the contact was U-Boat, the attack was made. The first pattern was fired, but still the contact was strong, although appearing to sink slightly. The second attack was made and suddenly the sightseers became quiet and watchful. Was that an oil patch on the surface? At that time I was too busy reloading the depth charge throwers to be able to take a peep at anything. Somebody said that they saw the stern of a submarine rise out of the water and sink back in again. once again all our work seemed to have been in vain, for the Captain said we could not in any way claim a kill because there was no tangible evidence that what we had attacked was a U-Boat, but could quite possibly have been a whale.

On the 9th June, "KENYA, "BEDOUIN" and the Polish manned 'Hunt' class destroyer "KUJAWIAK" detached from the convoy, leaving H.M.S. "LIVERPOOL" in charge, and set course for Gibraltar for refuelling and reammunitioning, and set speed to arrive there in darkness so as not to be seen from the shore, because Spain was then known to be a huge nest of German spies, our arrival being on the night of 10th June. What a sight, seeing all those lights on the Spanish shores.

It was still thought that our final destination was to be West Africa, but when on the morning of 11th June all our confidential books were bagged up and taken ashore, some uncertainty began to enter our minds. Thus, after taking on fresh provisions, water, etc, we prepared once more for sea, slipping out after dark. Our course eventually easterly.

Morning of the 12th June saw us once again in the company of the convoy, steering east, but what an almighty escort there was. The Captain cleared lower deck to speak to us (in the fore mess deck), and it was then we found our real destination - Malta! We were part of a force to try to get much needed supplies to Malta, and it appeared that a similar convoy was trying to get through from Alexandria.

Looking out at the escorting force, for by now, six merchantmen, "TROILUS", "BURDWAN", "CHANT", "ORARI", "TANINBAR", and the tanker "KENTUCKY", were the battleship H.M.S. "MALAYA", two aircraft carriers, H.M.S. "EAGLE" and H.M.S. "ARGUS", and the cruisers H.M.S. "KENYA" carrying the flag of Vice Admiral Curteis, H.M.S. "LIVERPOOL", H.M.S. "CHARYBD-

IS", and the A.A. cruiser H.M.S. "CAIRO". Having seen that little lot, we on destroyers thought that if there were to be any enemy hanky-panky, it would be the big 'uns that would catch it first.

Captain (D) in H.M.S. "ONSLOW" took up point position on the port wing of the screen, while H.M.S. "BEDOUIN" took her position at point on the starboard screen, being the Half-Leader (2nd I/C), while away either side of these two the other destroyers formed into an enormous arrowhead formation. These ships were H.M.S. "MATCHLESS", H.M.S. "MARNE", H.M.S. "PARTRIDGE", H.M.S. "ITHURIAL", H.M.S. "ICARUS", H.M.S. "ESCAPADE", H.M.S. "ANTELOPE", H.M.S. "VIDETTE", H.M.S. "WISHART, H.M.S. "WESTCOTT", H.M.S. "WRESTLER", the four Hunt class destroyers H.M.S. "BLANKNEY", H.M.S. "BADSWORTH", H.M.S. "MIDDLETON", and the Polish ship "KUJAWIAK". Astern of the convoy came the four minesweepers H.M.S. "HEBE", H.M.S. "SPEEDY", H.M.S. "RYE" and H.M.S. "HYTHE", plus six motor launches. Temporarily attached, the fast minelayer H.M.S. "WELSHMAN", which took up station with the main body of the convoy.

H.M.S. "EAGLE's" fighter aircraft consisted of about a dozen Hurricanes, which had been specially adapted for use on aircraft carriers, while H.M.S. "ARGUS" carried eight or nine Fairy Fulmars. This was the sum total of fighter aircraft we had to protect the convoy, although only about a third of those would ever be airborne at any one time. Apart from these, for anti U-Boat and scouting, the famous Fairy Swordfish, commonly known as 'Stringbags', were airborne from dawn to dusk, with fighter escorts of course.

The Spanish coast still remained visible on our port side, so it became obvious that this little lot had been spotted and reported to some fat German bigwig when 'Snoopy Joe' appeared on the scene, naturally at a very safe distance and constantly reporting our position.

Saturday 13th June dawned bright and clear, 'Snoopy Joe' appeared far away as usual, sending back a continuous stream of reports throughout the day, while in the convoy there were submarine scares, with the escorting warships taking counter measures. As the day wore on, it became increasingly obvious that before long we were going to be in the middle of a whole heap of trouble.

Sunday 14th June. Small groups of aircraft began to appear, with some high-level bombing, which was ineffective. We now knew we were well within the range of enemy bombers, and the convoy escorts were deployed accordingly. The Fleet destroyers in the screen opened into a very wide semi-circle around the main body of the convoy to act as the first defence against the attacking enemy planes, if we could. The fighter aircraft from the carriers had been in contact with, and skirmished with marauding enemy aircraft from practically first light.

At approximately 10.00, the raids started in earnest. A concoction of high-level bombers and torpedo bombers, all coming in from practically all points of the compass. In this first big attack, H.M.S. "KENYA" let fly with a broadside of every gun she carried, the result being, with a following wind to aid the illusion, that she was completely enveloped in her own gun smoke, and from our position aboard "BEDOUIN", looked as if she had been hit. One can well imagine how relieved we felt when she emerged from the smoke cloud unharmed. "KENYA" then went on firing other similar broadsides at the approaching torpedo bombers, apparently downing several.

In a later attack by torpedo bombers, some got through the barrage and H.M.S. "LIVERPOOL" was hit port side aft, damage being done to her port after engine, and she slowed and turned out of line, listing to port. Somehow she managed to limp back to Gibraltar, apparently unmolested by enemy planes who were too intent on the convoy to worry about her. At the same time the merchant ship "TANINBAR" was hit and sank.

During all this, the fighters from our carriers were having a whale of a time. Although in the end we had lost about three fighters to the enemy, they had put up a very spirited defence of the convoy, and were able to claim a number of downed aircraft of the enemy.

Soon after seeing the "LIVERPOOL" turn away, down at the stern and listing to port, a high level attack started, and we watched as H.M.S. "WELSHMAN" came under attack. She dodged a stick of bombs by doing a high speed turn, and streaking away, then turning back to retake her position in the convoy. During all this, we in destroyers, had been playing our small part by having a go at any enemy plane that got close enough. I understand that the Official Photographer we were carrying managed to lose three good cameras through being too anxious to get the best shots he could, and all through getting too close to the business end of our 4.7" guns. The blast as they fired blew the camera's out of his hands.

As the day wore on some of the enemy planes, such as torpedo bombers, made their getaway by flying low over the sea and between the destroyers on the screen, who dared not fire at him for fear of hitting one of their own ships. This problem was eventually sorted out by firing at low flying aircraft at an angle over the stern from a safe bearing on each quarter, and again from a safe bearing before the beam to dead ahead.

During the afternoon, a one man raft was sighted ahead, and in it an enemy pilot, who, once within hailing range started frantically waving his arms at us. Some wag on one of the forwards guns, using the boat hailing routine, shouted out as the poor chap passed by, "Passing". (At night when a boat is approaching a ship, it will be hailed by the call "Boat Ahoy". If not calling at that ship, the boat's coxswain will answer with "Passing").

As dusk approached, there came a sudden flurry of attacks from high level, torpedo and dive bombers, but ships' gunfire effectively beat them off. Once more at about 21.00, dive bombers appeared again, but again no luck for them. H.M.S. "WELSHMAN" had been detached, and was doing a fast run into Malta, loaded I gather, with necessary ammunition for the garrison at Malta.

Now, at about 21.30, it was the time for Force X to break away from the main body and escort the convoy into Malta. This Force consisted of the A.A. Cruiser H.M.S. "CAIRO", Senior Officer, the destroyers H.M.S. "BEDOUIN", Senior Officer Destroyers, H.M.S. "MATCHLESS", H.M.S. "MARNE", H.M.S. "PARTRIDGE", H.M.S. "ITHURIAL", the four Hunt class destroyers H.M.S. "BLANKNEY", H.M.S. "BADSWORTH", H.M.S. "MIDDLETON", and the Polish ship "KUJAWIAK", the four minesweepers H.M.S. "HEBE", H.M.S. "SPEEDY", H.M.S. "RYE", H.M.S. "HYTHE", and the motor launches. To cap it all, we still had five merchant ships.

We were at Action Stations all night. There had been a signal that a force of cruisers and destroyers had been spotted on longitude 18° east and steaming south-easterly, so they would have proved no problem, except the fact that somehow 10° of longitude had been added to the sighting. That we found out the following morning.

Throughout the night we could see flares being dropped, which as far as we could make out, meant that we were being shadowed. After the Force had rounded Cap Bon, at approximately 02.15, what appeared to be an enemy vessel came in sight. The Fleet destroyers, "BEDOUIN", "MATCHLESS", "MARNE", "PARTRIDGE", and "ITUHURIAL" opened fire, but almost immediately the cease fire was given by "BEDOUIN". It was thought that we had opened fire on the wreck of H.M.S. "HAVOC".

Monday 15th June. Apart from the flares, nothing untoward had happened since we had fired at what we though was the wreck of H.M.S. "HAVOC". As dawn broke we were looking forward to a nice hot cup of tea and something to eat. Alas, it was not to be. A long range fighter reported a force of cruisers and destroyers right across our path. Sure enough, at 06.30 there they were, two cruisers and five destroyers. Range, about 10 miles.

At the moment of sighting the enemy force, H.M.S. "CAIRO" turned the convoy away, and assisted by the four Hunts and minesweepers, laid a smoke screen around the merchantmen. The cruisers had by then opened fire on the convoy, but with no success, and the "CAIRO" fired her dual purpose 4" guns, more by way of boosting morale than any hope of landing a shot on one of the enemy.

The five Fleet destroyers, in two sub-divisions, had turned toward the cruisers. The first sub-division consisted of "BEDOUIN" I/C, "MATCHLESS" and "MARNE", carrying a combined punch of 18 x 4.7" guns and 12 torpedoes. The second sub-division, consisting of "PARTRIDGE" and "ITHURIAL", carried between them 4 x 4" and 4 x 4.7" guns and 8 torpedoes.

Speed increased to 32 knots, and with the enemy now on our port side, we became the centre of attraction for the two cruisers. As leading ship, we in "BEDOUIN" were the first to get fired at. I, as communication number on the torpedo tubes, had a fair view of some of what was happening. The two lines of destroyers were weaving in order to throw off the enemy gunnery, quite successfully at the beginning, although early on our Battle Ensign, which had been hoisted to the masthead, came down with the top of the mast when it was struck by a rather over the top shot.

"MATCHLESS" sustained a hit and weaved out of line for a few minutes, and then returned to the fray. "MARNE" was also hit, but we could not see how much damage had been done. Every so often a small shudder ran through the ship as shots hit her. Our speed dropped to 28 knots, communications suddenly ceased, and we realised some vital damage had been received. It had. A shell had come in through the ship's side just above the water line, at an angle to the bow, into the Lower Power Room, demolishing the 24 volt switchbo-ard, two 24 volt generators, narrowly missing the two 24 volt batteries, wrecked the 200 volt switchboard, and gone right through the watertight bulkhead into No. 1 boiler room exploding on the steam fan. This caused the boiler room to be closed down, thus reducing our speed. Amazingly, there were no casualties from all this.

Up on deck there had been casualties, but at this stage, very light. As the torpedo tubes were trained on the port beam, all ready for firing, I was positioned rather uncomfortably close to the four 750lb warheads. Overhead there came the constant moan of enemy shells, while every few minutes large spouts of water erupted where shots had fallen short, or one would hear a short moan quickly followed by a thud as one passed over the top. One such shot fell just clear of the starboard side right behind the tubes, and exploding on impact with the water sent shrapnel flying. Three of the tubes crew sustained injuries with that one. One had a fractured ankle, one a piece of shrapnel in his back close to his spine at the base, and the third had a piece of his left thigh removed.

When the action started, the range had been some 20,000 yards. The high speed was necessary to get as close to the enemy as possible in the shortest time possible. Opening fire was the Captain's option. As it was we eventually opened fire at 8,800 yards, and not, as expected on the cruisers, but as the hunter does with geese, on the last destroyer of the line. Having given that one a right shaking up, attention was turned to the next in line, and he was sorted out, retiring, as had the first victim of our wrath, hurt, badly hurt. Our attention then turned to the cruisers, and by switching from one to the other frequently, rather upset their equilibrium.

With the range rapidly closing and, as I later found out, all our guns firing by local control, the time would soon arrive when it would be the time for the torpedoes to be fired. Watching the port wing of the bridge for any sign that all might not be well at the T.C.O.'s position, I saw the flash as a shell hit the gunnery director tower. In an instant I realised that the T.C.O.'s position could well have been wiped out, and yelled to the L.T.O. in charge of the tubes crew that we go into local control.

The tactic of rapidly switching targets had paid off, for we were now only 3,000 yards from the cruisers and beginning to make the turn to starboard to fire torpedoes. At this stage the T.C.O. appeared coming from the bridge, a rather shaken looking person, who as he reached the tubes, called out for us to fire locally as our sights came on target.

As the ship heeled in the turn, the bulk of the enemy cruisers loomed large before us. It seemed as if one could almost step aboard them. Frantic figures could be plainly seen running about on their decks. As one person put it, you could see the whites of their eyes.

Slowly the targets came into our sights and the L.T.O. calmly chanted 'fire one', 'fire two', 'fire three', 'fire four', 'all tubes fired', just as if it were a practice run. Unfortunately it was for real, for as the last tiddler left the tubes, both cruisers fired a full broadside together. Fifteen shells, winged their way well above our heads and splashed down a long way from us, but number sixteen found it's mark, landing just aft of the tubes and exploding in the gearing room, thus putting both engines out of action in one fell swoop.

As the ship slowly came to a halt, the enemy cruisers were seen to be making a rapid turn to port away from us, and increasing speed as well. Well! Who wants to hang around when there are several tin fish belting toward them at 45 knots? Despite the damage received, and the fact that we were now a sitting target for any enemy ship that liked to dare to approach close enough, the job of the five Fleets had been done - to turn the enemy away from the convoy.

"MATCHLESS", "MARNE" and "ITHURIAL" carried on after the retreating enemy ships until recalled by "CAIRO". "PARTRIDGE" came alongside and finally took "BEDOUIN" in tow. "PARTRIDGE" had received damage which reduced her steaming capacity to a mere 18 knots, but had enough power to tow "BEDOUIN" at about 8 knots.

After receiving our disabling hit, we who were free and able to do something set about making the depth charges safe and ditching them. All explosive materials kept in the explosives room (torpedo and depth charge), which was situated in the superstructure immediately aft of the torpedo tubes, detonators, primers and the such like, were all passed over to Davy Jones' Locker.

When this very necessary piece of work had been completed, it was time for us to take stock of the damage received. The port side of the ship from upper deck to water line looked more like a pepper pot than a ship's side. Two shells had come in just above the water line on the lower mess deck, and had passed right through the ship, leaving gaping holes and the wreckage of ships-side lockers strewn about. Shrapnel had caused most of the other damage, with ports smashed and hanging off their hinges.

On the upper deck, we had received a shot bang on the bullring on the bows, which had curled the steel deck up like and opened sardine tin. Going aft, the topmast, which had come down early in the engagement, had dropped across the whaler, smashing it in two. On the port side, the motorboat had a large lump torn out of the keel, and the davits had been hit by shrapnel and were jammed. One shot had entered through the Officers Heads, passed through the hatch of the depth charge magazine, narrowly missing a full stock of depth charges carried there, careered through the Engineer Officer's cabin and out through the ship's side before exploding. Probably the worst hit of the lot was a direct hit on the Radar Cabin, situated on the flag deck, which is the deck directly under the bridge, which killed everybody in the cabin and one signalman on the flag deck.

There were many other areas of damage, the ammunition ready use lockers on X gun deck had been hit, with as much shrapnel damage aft as forward. Other incidents I have previously quoted. Those available were already trying to rectify some of this damage, while the wounded were being attended and the dead sewn up in hammocks weighted with solid shot ready for burial at sea. For doing this last job, those so occupied received an extra tot of rum.

In the midst of all this, the photographer was dashing around trying to get pictures of as much damage as he could, and asking members of the crew to pose by the damage wearing broad grins. Who felt like smiling at a time like that? Admittedly, we were still afloat, which was something, and we were under tow, but how long would it be before somebody on the other side tried to make the most of our predicament? Not long, we guessed.

The rum ration came up a bit early, and was greatly appreciated, but when chef called us for dinner, that was the end. Nothing could be cooked, so good old chef provided us with corned beef sandwiches. As far as I was concerned, a bully beef sandwich did not fit into the pattern of things. A couple of bites and over the side with it.

Whilst under tow, the four Hunts passed us at speed, apparently making toward the cruiser force. Unbeknown to us, during the action, the convoy had been attacked by aircraft, and the tanker and one of the merchantmen had been badly damaged enough for the tanker to be taken in tow, but the "CHANT" had sunk. In a later attack, a second merchant ship became disabled. This one was "BURDWAN" who had by then prepared to scuttle.

One of the Hunts, H.M.S. "BADSWORTH", and the minesweeper H.M.S. "HEBE" had been detailed to scuttle both the tanker "KENTUCKY" and the "BURDWAN". Later in the afternoon, enemy aircraft took over from our ships and conveniently torpedoed the two ships and sank them.

While all the above was taking place with the convoy, "PARTRIDGE" was still towing "BEDOUIN", when from nowhere two cruisers and two destroyers appeared. The cruisers seemed to take no notice of us, obviously they had a better target in sight. The destroyers however, tried an approach, but "BEDOUIN" opened fire on them, and off they hopped, laying smoke.

"PARTRIDGE", taking orders from "BEDOUIN", slipped the tow and proceed to drop smoke floats around "BEDOUIN". We also set off our own smoke floats, and as we were just moving under a little power from one engine, were managing to spread a smoke screen about ourselves. All available ready use ammunition was taken from other mountings and transferred to 'B' mounting. Meanwhile, all attempts to haul in the half shackle of cable now hanging down over the bows came to nought, because it had become snagged up in the rolled up section of deck, and most likely caught up in the wreckage of what was left of the paint shop. So it was left to dangle.

Once again one of the enemy destroyers tried to creep through his smoke screen, only to be met with a nicely placed pair of shots. Back into the smoke he went. This cat and mouse game continued, but the enemy seemed very reluctant to make a bold dash in to finish us off. Perhaps what had happened during the initial engagement had cooled their ardour, nobody likes to see their own side taking a good tousing.

Somewhere between 14.15 and 14.30 "BEDOUIN" was attacked by a torpedo bomber. Due to the very slow forward movement, the torpedo struck at the bulkhead separating the engine room from the gearing room on the starboard side. The bomber came off second best as well, it was shot down by fire from our 20mm Oerlikon guns.

As the thump and shudder went through the ship, she first started to heel to starboard, but then came upright and began listing to port. This was the moment the Captain gave orders to abandon ship. Now came the moment of reckoning, for most of our life saving equipment had been destroyed in the action. However, one had to trust the Pussers issue blow-up life belt.

It is funny what one does in circumstances such as these. I can remember, having helped one of my injured chums out on to the upper deck, taking off my shoes and placing them neatly up against the galley bulkhead. By then the ship had listed over so far that the sea was about to spill on to the upper deck, so calmly climbing on to the guard rail, I then dived over the side, still wearing my tin hat believe it or not. Like everybody else I began to swim as fast as possible to reach a safe distance from the sinking ship.

Eventually I reached a small balsa raft, it could support eight men hanging on to the grab ropes. It was when the 16ft fast motorboat arrived loaded to overflowing, and full of holes, asking for something to bail out the boat with, that I was reminded that I still had my 'Battle Bowler' on, so over it went to where it could do best service.

Unless one has experienced it, one cannot realise or know the feeling and sense of utter loss as you watch the ship that has been your home and haven for so long, slide beneath the sea, taking with it some of your best chums.

As the ship slowly heeled over on to her port side, the Captain, last to leave, having made sure everyone alive had gone over the side, jumped from the bridge wing and swam to join the rest of us. Slowly, ever so slowly, the stern began to go under, as it sank from sight, the ship righted herself, then as the stern sank lower her bows lifted out of the sea and she stood vertical on her stern and hung there for a full minutes before gently sliding under the surface of the sea. Hardly a stir in the water as she slide to her final resting place, to become another unmarked War Grave.

All that was left to mark the passing of "BEDOUIN" was a patch of oil, which soon spread to engulf her survivors. Now we were able to stock of our position. Between some 215 survivors, there were one 16ft motor boat, 2½ Carley Rafts, two floatanets, two balsa rafts each capable of supporting eight men hanging on to the lifelines, a couple of lifebuoys and pieces of assorted wreckage.

Two of the lads who had sustained very severe injuries were supported until eventually both died from their wounds, and possible exposure, and they were allowed to drift away. The rest of us had to do the best we could to keep alive and not give in to the situation we found ourselves in. I eventually found myself on a floatanet, submerged up to my waist, but in the warm waters of the Mediterranean, that seemed of little consequence.

CHAPTER THREE

Rescue and Captivity

The isolated groups of survivors gradually drew together to form a solid black, oily large group. The chances of being picked up were infinitely greater by far when there is a large number together, rather than a number of small scattered groups, or even isolated boats.

The worst enemy at the moment was the thick, black oil fuel. It spread out and clung to the men in the water like so much tacky glue, making it an effort to swim even a small distance. It got into the eyes, and stung and burned, it clogged up nostrils making it hard to breathe properly. Every effort to clear or get clear of this glutinous mess came to nothing, it just clung on and followed, and as soon as movement stopped, surrounded the survivors once more.

Soon after the sinking, two large cruisers passed on one side of us at some 2 or 3 miles distant, and two destroyers passed the other side of us at about the same distance. These Italian ships were steaming at high speed, and seemed to have some definite object in view, and I can only think it was the destroyer H.M.S. "PARTRIDGE" they were after.

Then came the long wait, hoping that one of our own ships would come along and pick us up. The sun was hot overhead, but although the water was quite warm, soon it began to have a chilling effect. Unfortunately, there were so many men to so few pieces of life saving equipment, that for the most part we were half immersed in the sea, with no hope of getting dry, even for a short while.

Left alone, there was nothing to do, but watch out for a rescue ship and keep a sharp eye open in case any enemy aircraft saw us and took a dislike to us.

We could still see the columns of smoke rising from the burning ships disabled after the action, and several times German planes flew over, making for the burning wrecks, and even at that long distance, we could feel the thump of the bomb explosions through the water. It was just like being hit sharply in the stomach, although at that distance the raps were very light.

At one time three Me's came over and spotting us came in for a look. We all prepared to do a quick dive under the surface if necessary, but after a cursory glance, they sheered off, much to our relief.

The sun sank slowly below the horizon, and we were preparing to spend a long, sleepless night clinging to our pitiful rafts, and hoping that we would have the strength to hang on until morning. As the sun went down, so the evening breeze sprang up, making a small chop in the water, causing the oil to move about and splash us more.

Then, when hope had almost gone for a rescue, somebody spotted a hospital plane circling overhead, and as the plane spotted us, it came down and landed. The pilot indicated that a ship was not far away. However, he took aboard six of our men, then took off and, I suppose, signalled the position of us to the ship.

It was almost dark when a light coloured ship appeared over the horizon, giving us only a bows on view. At first it looked just like one of our 'Hunts', but as it drew nearer, we could see it was a hospital ship, and an Italian one at that.

The hospital ship hove to a short distance away, and lowered a couple of boats. As they pulled in among us, ready to take the badly wounded, three biplanes turned up, and without warning, as they were loaded with light bombs, dived on the hospital ship and started to release their bombs. These fell perilously close to the ship, and some fell among us, although with the appearance of the ship we had spread out quite a lot. Luckily, they caused neither casualties or damage to the hospital ship, and before they could come in for a second go at us, they were driven off by three Me.109's which appeared from out of the blue like guardian angels.

The hospital ship had made a hurried departure when the biplanes made the attack, but now they had been driven off, back it came and the work of rescue continued. I was one of the last to be picked up, being one of the furthest away from the ship. When I did manage to get to the ship's side, I had to be hauled aboard, I had no strength left, and I was paralysed from the waist down, due to the long immersion in the water.

It was a blessed relief to be aboard a ship once more, no matter it was an enemy craft. At least we were free of the clinging oil, and now we could strip off our sodden garments and, perhaps, warm up a bit. I used my underwear to wipe off as much oil as I possibly could, and then, in the nude, I joined the majority of the crew in the saloon.

There we sat through the long hours of the night, dozing now and then, but feeling the warm glow spreading through our bodies.

About dawn there came a terrific bang, waking us all from our doze, and the ship rocked enough to make us all start up in alarm. Panic stricken shouts from outside the saloon announced that the Italian crew had really got the wind up. The thought that came into my head was that the hospital ship had struck a mine, and I was preparing, in my mind, to start swimming for it again. However, the panic died down after a couple of minutes, and an Italian crewman came in to assure us that everything was alright.

At about 08.00 the ship tied up in the harbour of Pantelleria. A good hour later we were bade leave the saloon. We were not to be handed over to the island garrison.

As each of us left the saloon, we were given a blanket, except for those lucky ones who had been given an Italian Naval Uniform the night before when we had been picked up.

Thus, the great majority of us dressed only in a blanket, we were led ashore. A fleet of lorries awaited us, and into these we piled. The lorries were open ones, and seats had been arranged across the width of the lorries by using planks, and thus we had to sit, facing the rear, in true Italian style, always looking behind.

The drive was a slow one over pretty poor roads, and lined up all along the roadside were dozens of Italian officers and men, and some civilians, all armed with cameras, ready to take our photos as we passed.

I would like to know just how many photographs were spoiled that day. Just as someone would be about to click his shutter, so one of the lads gave the ‘V’ sign, and some did even worse. Many were the rude remarks passed about the Italians, and many the insults hurled at them.

The ordeal of the ride came to an end at last, and we were set down between two huts, rather like overgrown garden sheds, and about as airy and comfortable as one. These were to be our temporary quarters, half our numbers to each hut, officers included.

A water lorry was brought up, and we were provided with a green, clay like substance that we were told was SOAP! With this non-lathering substance we had to do the best we could to get the oil off our bodies. The water was lukewarm, probably the water lorry had been standing overnight loaded. Doing the best we could with the materials provided, we were then issued with some clothing, to wit, white Italian Naval uniform, without trimmings.

Somebody mentioned that we had not eaten for over 24 hours, then our Captain got on to the Officer in Charge, and demanded that we be fed. The feeding of us was handed over to the Italian Navy. I will say that, with their tender mercy, the food they gave us was the best we had during our entire stay as uninvited and not so welcome guests of Il Duce and the Italian Government.

About 17.00 that evening we had our first taste of Italian food. As far as I can remember it consisted of a small fish, but soaked in olive oil, a most ghastly concoction to our palates, a bowl of soup made from spaghetti and beans, a piece of cheese and a small bread roll. Black coffee was issued after the main part of the meal. To our rumbling and famished stomachs, it was indeed a meal worthy of a king, except of course the fish.

The major problem, now that we had been fed, was the call of nature and what, if any, provisions had been made for such. We soon knew what provisions had NOT been made for nature's calls.

In order to go to the lavatory, we had to call the guard, and he would only allow three men to go at a time. The latrine, we found, was the open beach and rocks.

The seriously wounded had been taken to the very large modern military hospital of Pantelleria, and the Ship's Doctor had gone there with them.

As darkness fell, we settled down to sleep, but the guards, some of whom were Italian sailors who spoke a few words of English, though the words they knew were not to be found in any English dictionary, decided to move in among us and try to talk. One or two of them were quite amusing, and as a result of this first night with them, a friendship, peculiar to those who go down to the sea in ships, was set up between British and Italian sailors. This was to last for the short duration of our stay.

Next on the list was the Italian Admiral Commanding, Pantelleria. His visit occasioned the issue of a packet of 20 cigarettes to each man, with the appropriate book of matches. A most humane and kind-hearted man, he enquired of our health and comfort, and if there was any small things he could do to help us. He was genuinely concerned about our welfare, and almost fell over himself to do anything he possibly could.

With our own Captain leading the complaints, the Admiral soon had a body of Italian soldiers building a sort of latrine out of bamboo poles high up on the rocks. Unfortunately, for the time being, the rule of only three at a time still stood.

The first signs of colds in the stomach and mild dysentery showed during the third day. This led to a constant queue remaining formed for visits to the latrine, and by the end of the day, a determined rush was made by all, disregarding the shouts and threats of the guard.s The result of this was that a couple of guards constantly kept a patrol by the rocks, while we could go and return as we pleased.

It was on the third day that I had to see the Italian doctor. My right foot had suddenly swollen to enormous proportions. After a bit of probing, the doctor decided that my foot would have to be lanced.

Motioning three of his biggest medical orderlies to lay hold of me, he then produced his bottle of local anaesthetic, grabbed hold of my foot and squirted on the freezing liquid. The situation was now thus. One orderly had my right leg firmly held, the second orderly was hanging on to my left arm for dear life, and the third orderly was trying to bury my face into his coat so that I could not see what was going to happen. Also, I learned later, to stop my wild and agonised screams piercing the air. Apparently, the Italian medical staff had only had Italian personnel to deal with up to now, and they were used to wild screams of heart-rending agony being emitted by their patients even for only treating a scratched finger.

So the pantomime was set. The doctor poised his rather blunt lancet. I had by then wriggled my head free enough to breathe freely and to see what was going on, much to the undisguised dismay of the doctor. However, taking a deep breath, he plunged his lancet into my foot, fully expecting me to give forth an unearthly, ear splitting scream of pure fright and agony, or at least burst into tears. The disbelief and amazement that showed in his face when nothing of the sort happened, was truly comical, and his amazement grew when I showed great interest in what was then oozing from my foot, and I had not even winced or flinched throughout the whole proceedings.

Our Ship's Doctor brought to us from the hospital the unhappy news that two of our Ship's Company had died there. One had died from gangrene on the brain, the shrapnel which had caused the wound still being embedded in his head. The other fellow had a fractured leg, but seemed to have lost the will to live, and simply faded away.

Those two deaths brought the total casualties to 32 from a ship's company of 241 officers and men. For the amount of punishment the ship took, this final total figure of fatalities was indeed a light one, but I am sad to say that some of my best friends were among those who sank to the ocean bed with the ship.

The Admiral was soon on the scene, offering his condolences to us over these two most recent deaths, I will go so far as to say he was almost in tears at the thought that two very brave English sailors had died whilst under his care, it was almost as if he had lost two of his own sons.

The days wore slowly past, the daily visits from the Admiral bringing a small spot of light relief to us, and our Captain being a tower of strength, organising sing-songs, and in general keeping our spirits up.

A week after our sinking, 22nd June 1942, wildly jubilant Italian soldiers came rushing towards us waving newspapers. Tobruk had fallen, and to the simple minds of the Italians, it seemed as if the war was as good as over, and there was nothing left bar the shouting.

The fall of Tobruk may have been uplifting to them, but to us it was decidedly disheartening. However, we did our best not to show it, and soon convinced the Italians that Tobruk was only a small victory, and it would not be very long before it was in British hands again.

Our time in Pantelleria had now come to an end, and we had to go to a transit camp in Sicily. Once more we were loaded on to lorries and driven down to the jetty, where we were met by the Admiral. He was in a state of extreme upset, he was losing his beloved British sailors. It was a very tearful farewell he bade us as we mounted the gangplank of the ship which was to take us to Sicily.

CHAPTER FOUR

For you the War is over!

Having been put aboard a transport at Pantelleria, the Italian army guards took over from the Naval guards and at first tried to put us in the ships hold. We, however, were not having that. We kip down on the upper deck. What would happen, we asked, if the transport were to be tin-fished by a British submarine. We wouldn't stand a chance in the hold. We got our way and stayed on the upper deck for the overnight trip to Trapani in Sicily.

On arrival at Trapani, we spotted the well burnt shape of an Italian destroyer in the harbour, looking as if she would be out of action for the foreseeable future. Going alongside a jetty, we were soon unloaded and placed in some lorries waiting there. The next stop would be the transit camp.

Arrival at the gates of the camp became another cause for us to raise our eyebrows. We were told to get in a column and when we marched through the gate to salute the sentry. Oh yes! says we, they'll get a salute alright, but it won't be any drill book salute. Well, they did get a variety of salutes, from a smart Royal Marine type in which the thumb was extended to reach the tip of the nose to rather rude type boy scout salutes. None of the Italians seemed to notice what we were doing.

The camp turned out to be three large tents, with space enough for a hundred men in each. Our bedding was to be bales of straw which we could spread out to form a mattress, drinking water came in large bottles containing about two gallons in each, and these had to be filled each day when the water tanker arrived.

Now we found out what the real rations were for P.o.W.'s. A simple case of "pani aqua". Pani or bread, consisted of a small roll, one of which had to last all day, and a watery vegetable soup at noon. Early morning meal consisted of a cup of coffee, or two if any remained after sharing it out.

The first thing we had to do was to get our hair clipped off. We had noticed that those who had arrived before us had become 'eggheads'. We had to look them in the face to know who was which.

This hair cutting was a blessing in disguise really, because it got rid of all the oil remaining in our rather clogged hair.

Again, in this camp, the sanitary system was a bit crude. For toilets, a long trench about five feet deep was first dug, and across it at intervals were placed thick branches for footrests and seats. After a time and constant complaints, a screen of long branches complete with leaves was placed around the trench. This stopped local yokels peeping at us from the perimeter wire. In no time at all these toilets became known as the sea boats, and all using them the sea boats crew. Well, when all the seats were occupied, we did look something like a boats crew, but without oars.

We were still suffering from our stomach rumblings, so the toilets were in constant use. At one time I was sitting behind the G.I., and he, out of the blue, said "My arse hole is sticking out that far you can cut washers off it". I think we all had sore backsides, a lack of toilet paper meant we had to use the next best thing, bunches of long grass. In the course of the three weeks we stayed in this camp, new trenches were dug a number of times and the old ones, now very smelly, were filled in.

Work was occasional and light. There was a malarial stream running through the field the camp was situated in, so they called on us to help them clear it a bit. We were given a daily dose of malaria tablets, not that we thought they did much good. Another source of annoyance were the various types of wild life, David Attenborough would have been in his element. Often one woke to the noise of someone thrashing about, having been awakened by a lizard or sometimes a snake slithering over them. Insects seemed to be four times the normal size there.

This malarial ditch became the innocent source of a form of amusement, one never quite knew what Italian, or should I say Sicilian, oddity one might find in it. Enormous dragonflies, lizards, toads and snakes were common, and at one time we found a rather large snail, and were just about to dispose of it when the Italian sentry guarding us rushed over yelling "Niente, niente" (no, no), then swiftly grabbing hold of a shovel, plonked the offending snail upon it, lit a small fire, and held shovel plus snail over the flames. Looking up at us he said, "Bueno, mungaria, bueno, bueno". (Good, food, good, good). We looked at him in disbelief and the next time we found a toad and a snake, asked him if he would like them too.

About the second or third day there a new face was introduced into our gathering. He was dressed exactly as we were, and spoke perfect English, too perfect in fact. He said, upon being questioned, that he was from another ship that had been sunk about the same time as "BEDOUIN" had, but we became suspicious of him. We had heard of plants being made in camps where there were newly captured prisoners, trying to find out anything useful to the enemy.

When he started to ask rather guarded questions of us, we only told him exactly what was already known by the Italians. A conference with our Captain and officers made us even more wary. Apparently he had first landed up with them, and they were too canny to say anything in his hearing, and counselled us to act as they had. The nett result was that after about a week of fruitless questioning, he vanished just as quickly as he had arrived. (None the wiser, we hoped).

Apparently, the Italians must have thought it a good idea if they could interest us in a real live Italian interpreter, so we were introduced to the one and only Mario. That was the only name we ever knew him by. According to him, he had lived in Chicago for 7 years, and that was how he came to speak such good (Trans-Atlantic) English. He was a cheerful soul, always smiling, though at times rather strained to do so, we just could not help ribbing him. As he told us, he would be with us as our interpreter until we reached the permanent camp.

Mario didn't mind in the least talking about his stay in America, and when asked why he returned to Italy, he honestly and most earnestly said that he was an Italian, and that he thought it was the proper thing to do and join the Italian Army. We forgave him for that. But more of Mario later.

It was here that we were issued with our first postcard to be sent to the Vatican, who would then send on the information to the War Office in London. This card was a printed one on which we were to put our names, rating and official number, and cross out those words which did not apply, eg. 'I am being well treated/ill treated', or 'well fed/starved', and the such like, so that in the end, the card would read that you were happy, well fed, well treated, had no complaints etc. The real message we got through later in the main camp.

It was through these messages from the Vatican that the first news of our fate filtered through to our families, reaching them some two or three weeks later. For obvious reasons, the news that the ship had been sunk was kept on ice at the Admiralty for at least three to four weeks, depending on circumstances, and I do know that the fate of the "BEDOUIN" did not become known to the general public for some four weeks after the sinking.

We were getting little or no news from the outside, and what we did get came from the Italians, and their propaganda department soon rendered the truth into a fairy story. According to them, the British troops were being massacred, to put it mildly, the Italian P.o.W. camps should have been overwhelmed by the numbers who were giving themselves up to the Italians, all according to the Ities. Reading between the lines it became obvious that the 8th Army had come to a halt somewhere and were becoming a confounded nuisance to the Axis forces.

In our low state of mind, though not of morale, these reports had a dampening effect on our spirits, but not for long. The orders came through for us to be forthwith removed to the main camp. Mario came round with the glad tidings, and tried to get us going with a sing-song, picking on ancient songs well past their gone off time. Well, let's face it, he had been out of America for nearly three years at least, so he could not have been up with the latest tunes, now could he? Of course, Mario had been trying without much success to get us going with sing-songs for several days, without much enthusiasm being shown to his choice of song. 'She'll be coming round the mountain' being his favourite song.

Came the great day when we left this makeshift camp. We were mustered with our scanty belongings, and marched out of the gate. Then came the big question, 'What, no transport?'. No! No transport, it would be foot slogging it for all the 14km to the railway station at Castelvetrano.

The train waiting for us looked like something out of a Western film. Apart from the locomotive looking as if it should have been drawing its old age pension, the coaches were definitely antique stock. It would appear that all railway stock in Sicily were throw-outs from mainland Italian stock. On embarking, we found that the coaches were third class, with wooden seats made from well varnished plywood and artistically patterned with small holes (similar to the old tram stock of the long departed London County Council).

One consolation here though, we could lower the windows and let in plenty of very fresh air once moving which, in the heat, we badly needed ..... and, for the matter, so did the guards.

Eventually the train started to move off, the asthmatic engine wheezing away and belching out clouds of black smoke, steam leaking out of almost every steam pipe and valve on the loco. This train certainly was not a sprinter attaining what seemed to be about 15 m.p.h. over what seemed hours. However, this momentous rate was doomed to end very shortly.

From the town of Castelvetrano we had passed into some reasonably fertile country, for although we did not realise it, we were here in the very fertile coastal strip and we soon found the train wending its way through citrus fruit orchards. At last, panting like a well winded, over fed pet pekinese, the train groaned to a halt bang in the middle of a lemon grove. Oh! What a delight to see all those lovely ripe lemons hanging from the tree branches.

The stopped train soon attracted the attention of a number of Sicilian youths, schoolboys and slightly older males. On seeing the train packed with what were obviously British prisoners of war, they all approached to within speaking distance and started to hurl insults at us. This was our opportunity. With the windows fully down, the air soon became full of invective being thrown at each other. It was when somebody, obviously in command of a slight knowledge of the Italian language, suddenly bawled out "Italiano bastardos" (that speaks for itself), that the action took a turn which was to our liking.

Those Sicilian youths just had to throw something at these insulting perky and war-like prisoners, and the ammunition was ready at hand. Yes, lemons! Plucking the lovely ripe fruit from the trees, they put up a bombardment which we thoroughly enjoyed, for through the carriage windows came manna from heaven, fresh fruit! Egged on by further insults from us, the youths kept up their bombardment for several minutes longer than they probably intended, and the result, enough fresh lemons to last us for a day or two, fresh fruit which we badly needed.

After a time the youths seemed to tire of trying to make us lose our tempers, and retired to a safe distance. Finally peace reigned, and the guards were able to sit back once more, breathing sighs of relief. They too had profited from the lemon throwing session, so they too were satisfied.

Finally the train got moving again, slowly puffing off through the orchard, and eventually reaching the coast. Mario, the interpreter, had, during the lemon throwing episode, at first been running up and down the coaches yelling for peace and quiet, but after a few near misses from ripe lemons, gave up. He too breathed a huge sigh of relief when it ended.

Dusk was well and truly upon us when at last we passed through Palermo Station. A stop, probably to fill the leaky old engines tank, and off we puffed again. Now we were advised by Mario to try to get some sleep as we would be travelling through the night, (but not very fast). The problem was, how does one sleep on these wooden seats, our stern ends were already sore, and no amount of shifting position would cure that, so we had to try the impossible.

When dawn broke, we could see that we were close to the coast and running through some rugged country. Tired, sore and fed up, we almost cheered when Mario came to tell us to get our gear together as we would be detraining shortly at Messina.

After being cooped up in uncomfortable coaches for around twenty hours, we arrived at Messina, sleepless and weary, bleary eyed and very bad tempered. It was a great relief to get off that train and be able to breathe some reasonably fresh air and stretch our legs. Sore and stiff as we were then, we felt the effort of moving to be worth every creak of our bones.

Soon we were gathered into some semblance of order and marched to the ferry. On embarking we were led to the open sun deck and gathered together in a huddle away from the rest of the passengers, who had been staring at us as if we were some sort of monsters from the deep. When told by the guards that we were 'Inglese' (English), there were gasps of utter surprise from a number of them. Apparently, the Italian propaganda machine, to the civil population, had made us look like two headed ogre with four arms who ate small children for breakfast and adults for dinner. They were astonished to find we were ordinary human beings.

Now the fun began. Not being in good humour, it was the last straw when Mario, obviously with good intentions, asked us to gather round and sing a few songs. He started the ball rolling with his version of 'She'll be coming round the mountain' a song of which we were all heartily sick, and getting very little response, tried another old song well past its 'sell by' date, to which he only got loud groans. Then came the perfect squelch. A voice from the crowd started singing 'Oh, oh, Antonio', but substituting Mario for Antonio, and soon all of us were singing at the tops of our voices

Oh, Oh, Mario, he's gone away,

left me on my ownio, all on my ownio.
I'd like to meet him with his ice-cream cart,
then up will go old Mario,
ice-cream cart and all!

After that we were left to our own devices, which meant to enjoy in peace whatever we could of the sea crossing to the Italian mainland, hoping all the time that a British warship would appear and rescue us.

The crossing of the Straits of Messina (roughly about the same as from Cowes to Southampton) was uneventful, and we finally landed just to the north of Reggio di Calabria, and were taken to a railway station at Villa San Giovanni, where a train awaited us in the sidings. A look told us the worst, Third Class travel again. More wooden seat agony and stuffy coaches, and how long was this journey to be?

After being fed and watered, the time being somewhere around noon, we settled down to what comfort(?) we could manage as the train started its journey north. The only real comfort was being able to view the rather flat Italian coastal plain as the train took the coast line. The train kept a steady speed, and I noticed that this section of track was electrified with overhead catenary wires. No wheezy steam engines on this part liable to break down without notice.

The train kept its steady speed as we passed through numerous small villages and towns whose names it was rather too difficult to read, and the monotonous sound of wheels on rail had a rather soporific effect. Most of us falling into a doze for short periods of time, only to waken with a start as an extra heavy lurch by the coach took its toll on our sore rears.

Dusk came and in the distance we could see what appeared to be a flickering fire high up a hill side. When the train drew closer we could see it was Mount Vesuvius in high spirits, having erupted earlier in the year. Shortly after, we drew into Naples, stopping for about half an hour before moving off into the night again.

Now, with blinds down and lights extinguished, we could not see where we were going, nor take note of any town or village name along the way. We realised we would have to stay aboard the train another night, if we were not to be set down at a camp close at hand, which did not seem likely. The journey at this stage came to an end around midnight at Rome Station. Most of us were in some form of sleep by that time, so the cessation of motion did not awaken those asleep.

We were awakened not long before dawn and given hot coffee and a bread roll (a whole days ration). Soon the train was on its way again. This time, with the blinds rolled up, we were able to take notice of where we were going. A long string of well known places rolled by such as Civitavecchia, Livorno, Pisa - where we could see the famous leaning tower from the train, La Spezia, finally coming to a halt at Chiavari.

We were detrained and herded into army lorries. Mario was still with us, although the guards had been relieved by guards from the main camp. It was early evening now, and we were wondering how far it was to the camp. The exact distance turned out to be 14km and, on arrival we were herded into a building just off the road.

Enter the Camp Commandant, Mario called us to attention and turning to the Big Man, who used a walking stick and had a pronounced limp, chopped him off a smart salute, well, smart for an Italian, made his report and then ordered us to stand at ease. The Commandant began his set piece, arms waving, walking stick shaken, his voice getting louder and louder. Watching him we were asking each other what we had done to merit this ticking off since we had only just arrived, albeit reluctantly.

Without warning, the Commandant stopped yelling and stepped back. Mario took his place. Clearing his throat he started to speak. "The Colonel Commandant, says if you all behave yourselves and do not break any of the camp rules and do not try to escape, you will have a good time in this camp. Of course, if you misbehave and try to escape, you will be severely punished. I wish you goodnight and a happy stay in this camp."

Well, what do you make of that? We had already named the Commandant 'Hopalong' although we found out later that he had been wounded in the First World War whilst fighting alongside British troops in 1915. We also found out that he tended to be pro-British, and was very fair and did whatever he could for us prisoners.

After saying his little piece, Mario then wished us 'All the best', said goodbye and disappeared in the same general direction as the Camp Commandant. That was the last we saw of Mario, though in later days we did wonder where he had gone and what he was doing.

The camp guards now took over completely, and we were formed up into a rather untidy, straggling column and taken across the main road, down a path and across a wooden bridge, through the main gate of the camp to a couple of huts which were in need of inhabitants, Numbers 25 and 26. We split up here and took the hut of our choice. Each was supposed to house 100 men with double bunks along each side and at the end. An Army corporal was in occupation, and he was to be the N.C.O. in charge of the hut, so he had his own private room inside the entrance.

Hot coffee had been laid on, which was very welcome. I had chosen hut 26 and secured a lower bunk. As it was now dark, the lights came on, two miserable bulbs rated at about 25 watts. There was barely enough light to see where you were going in the gangway. There was only one thing to do and that was to turn in and sleep, if you could. None of us saw anything of the camp that night.

Our corporal had tried to give us some idea of the camp routine when we arrived, but we had to wait till morning to find out all about it. I suppose we, as British matelots, had always thought of the Italians as being a bit thick, but when it came to the morning and evening counts, we found out how thick a large number of the Italian Militia were. Even counting in two's some of these yokels in uniform could only get as far as ten before stopping to think what came after. The only intelligent ones were the sergeants and sergeant-majors.

After the early morning coffee and count, we were at liberty to wander around the camp for a while. We had been advised that wood for brewing was at a premium, and that outside walks had been arranged for the inmates to collect wood. To get on one of these walks, one had to get to the gate as early as possible, because only a limited number were allowed out at any one time. However, being dressed in Italian matelots rig, we were immediately given priority for the first week or so.

Just going on one of these wood collecting walks was an eye-opener in itself. We could see the poverty around us, the peasant life these people led. There were obviously many shortages of essentials, and a good nourishing diet was one of those shortages. We also noticed that these peasants did not show any hatred for us being there, there was no antagonism in any of their faces, they all seemed fed up with the war.

CHAPTER FIVE

Camp P.G. 52, Military Post 3100

It did come as a mild surprise to find out our camp's address. It was - Campo Concentramento Priggionare di Guerre 52, Posta Militare 3100. Quite naturally we asked what we were doing in a concentration camp. But, of course, the title of the camp only meant P.o.W. - concentration of - camp. All this large and flowery title became reduced to Camp P.G. 52, P.M. 3100.

It did not take very long for the local Italian Army Doctor to realise that he had some fresh blood to let. We had been in the camp about ten days, when we were told to muster at the gate and be marched to the Infirmary. There, we were to endure the first round of a jab that was a cocktail of several potent brews which were supposed to ward off almost any germ one could think of.

Having reached the Infirmary and reported our presence, we formed up in one long single file, and we who were a fair way back in the queue, could see those who had gone before us coming out of the door and in to the sun drenched courtyard, some to fall flat on their faces, others to stagger to a spot by the wall and slowly slide down into a sitting position, faces looking like death. One or two managed to walk out without staggering, and sit down by the wall without flopping down. It made us waiting to go in, wonder just what witches brew they were injecting into everybody.

Getting as far as the door to the surgery, we could then see what was going on. Just inside the surgery door, there stood an Italian medical orderly, with a handful of what I can only describe as cotton waste. This cotton waste had been liberally soaked in iodine, and as we came in the door, he grabbed us by the arm, swung us round and painted a bulls-eye on our chests. Then we were pushed over to where another orderly stood clutching another handful of cotton waste, and in between us and the farther medic stood an Italian doctor with the most villainous pair of crossed eyes anyone could wish not to see. This doctor, grasping a poised hypodermic syringe as if it were a dart, scoring a bulls-eye on each of our now not so manly chests. The second orderly pulled each one forward, swabbed his chest and then shoved each one of us on our way. I, like many others before me, came out into the sunshine, and then went down like a pole-axed bull. This was the one and only time a jab has put me out for the count. This whole performance was repeated a fortnight later when we had the second whack.

Perhaps it would be as well to give some idea of what the camp layout looked like. It was set in a valley, with one side of the camp facing the river which flowed down from the hills. On this side, which was on a diagonal from the front proper of the camp, had, next to the wire, the toilets, a rather crude arrangement of stone or slate slabs laid down as foot-rests (if that is the term), with a gap in between them over which one would squat and hope not to over balance, the sole attempt at privacy being to have large slabs between each trap and one at the back to stop people from seeing one from the road which ran alongside the river at that point. Underneath ran a large gulley, down which water was flushed every so often, usually first thing in the morning. The whole thing stank to high heaven, the sewage running out and down the bank into the river.

Parallel, and just a few feet away, were the Italian style baths. These consisted of a single pipe with holes drilled into it at intervals so that when the water was turned on it came out in a thin dribble, I cannot describe it as being any more. From that pipe we had to draw our water for drinking and brewing, wash and bathe ourselves and do such washing of clothes as we could. Hence, somebody would always be on look-out for when the water came on, and a loud hail would be given, "Water's on!" and a mad rush would ensue.

Going towards the main gate from the toilets and wash place, the wire hedged in a piece of ground just big enough to be a quarter size parade ground, and ended at the main gate. There it turned almost 90° to pass down the side of the camp cook house, canteen (for when we had any spare camp lira to spend), and a recreation hall, which became, eventually, a theatre for our camp plays etc.

The river had turned away from the camp just past where the main gate was situated, and then after a couple of hundred yards turned back again, the kink in the river's course leaving a wide grassy area behind the recreation hall. Going past the end of the recreation hall, the wire came back to the path, and there stood a gate across the path. This path, beyond the gate, led to the diesel generator house, and the infirmary, where dentistry as well as other devilish practices were performed. Well, judging by the awful moans and groans, and heart rending screams of pure mortal agony that were emitted from that place when any Italian militia were being operated on, one would have thought it was a torture chamber of the middle ages.

The perimeter wire now extended from the gate onward up a gentle slope to the back of the camp, turned 90° left and carried on to join with the perimeter wire from the main gate via toilets/wash place. Beyond the wire the ground rose steadily up and ever steeper to the top of the hill, a hill covered with lush green grass, bushes and trees.

In the enclosed space lay an assortment of huts, laid out in lines rising to the rear wire. Some were single deck, 100 men huts, others were double deckers housing about the same number. If I remember rightly, there were five or six rows, each row of varying length, housing a total of about 4,000 prisoners.

The generator supplying the camp with its electricity, was a rickety old job, very petulant, and liable to pack up without so much as a by your leave. Worse still, the shed it was housed in had been put in the field alongside the pathway to the infirmary, and at a lower level than the path, some two feet lower in fact and with the door facing the path. This comedy of errors led to many a sudden blackout, during the winter months especially. The supply cables from the generator to the camp were all carried on telegraph poles, which led to more funny business at a later date in this chronicle.

At this time in history, the perimeter wire consisted of coils of barbed wire wound on to trestles so that the coils stood about four feet high. Inside at the usual distance of a yard (or was it a metre?) ran the trip wire, raised to about knee high, beyond which nobody was supposed to venture. Sentry boxes were placed all around the perimeter at set intervals, close enough for the sentries to speak to each other without using a loud hailer. Perimeter lights were placed by each sentry box (so that the duty officer could see whether the sentries were awake or not) and at more frequent intervals between the boxes.

The gate across the entrance appeared to be the Italian version of a five bar gate, and knowing the Italian military of those days, had probably been half-inched from some local farmer's cart track to his farm. This was the one and only access to and from the camp compound. A sentry was posted there, complete with sentry box for him to hide in when no officers were about, or it rained. The sentry could very often be seen from our side of the wire, having a crafty smoke, obviously thinking he could not be seen by anyone of importance. Sometimes though, an officer or senior N.C.O. would come in from the infirmary side of the camp and catch the blissfully ignorant sentry unawares, when there would erupt an awe inspiring round of arm waving, loud shouting, and the N.C.O. or officer literally jumping up and down in rage. Obviously, the loud roars of laughter from us did not improve tempers very much on the other side of the wire.

We had been in the camp for about a month, and us matelots still only had the white Italian Navy uniform to wear, and when queuing up for a wood collecting walk were astonished to be singled out and sent back. The order had come from above that no British Naval personnel were to be let out of camp under any circumstances. The reason became clear very soon when we heard that a British submarine or submarines, had been operating off Genoa and making a perfect pest of themselves. To add insult to injury, a couple of British cruisers had nipped in under cover of dark and audaciously bombarded Genoa, causing havoc to the harbour.

About this time, one of the crew had managed to get an Italian magazine from somewhere, and sprawled across a centre page spread, an aerial photograph of "BEDOUIN" lying on its side not long before she finally slid beneath the waves. The damage she had received showed up clearly, including the gaping hole where the torpedo dropped by the aircraft had hit. The next time I saw that photo was when I went into a newsagent and bookshop in Shanklin, Isle of Wight, in 1981 and picked up a book entitled '2,194 Days of War', which happened to be marked at half price. Naturally, seeing that photo I bought the book.

By now we had fallen into the camp routine, such as it was, but the two main events of the week were the issuing of the Red Cross parcels. The allowance was one parcel per man per week, but to even things out so that everybody got something at each issue, we paired up and shared the two parcels. If I remember, the issues of parcels were made every Tuesday and Friday.

Whilst on the subject of parcels, we were allowed one personal parcel from our family once every three months, but cigarette parcels were allowed ad lib. The bare fact of that was that there were so many clubs, charities, friends and relations and other organisations all willing and able to send cigarettes that there was in fact no stopping them. With the personal parcel from family only, we asked them that at first they sent items of clothing such as socks and razors (safety) complete with blades, butterfly type tin openers, and some small amount of chocolate, after which the parcels should contain as much chocolate as possible after the other required items asked for were packed. i think the weight of the parcel was a maximum of 14lbs. sent at special rate.

Work in the camp literally did not exist. Sometimes there would be a call that a working party was required to bring in rocks from the river, mainly to make some decent paths around the camp, because at the first downfall of rain, even if only for a few minutes, the place became a quagmire.

On these stone lifting operations, the pace of movement became what was then known as the 'Chiavari Shuffle'. This meant in reality taking an enormous length of time to place one foot in front of the other, or moving at half snail speed. Oft times we would get a guard who wanted more speed, which usually resulted in an argument which the guard invariably lost. At other times the guard would slow us down even more, muttering "Piano, piano" (slow, slow) as we struggled along with the smallest rock we could find clutched to our bodies. One guard who wanted more speed actually made a threatening move with his rifle with bayonet attached when we ignored his plea, but soon made conciliatory gestures when he found he was completely surrounded by young gentlemen frowning in disbelief and holding rocks in their hands with arms in the throwing, rocks of, position.

During this period of haphazardness, the proper perimeter wire had been put up, so that we now had a ten foot double fence between us and the outside world. Best of all a Red Cross issue of clothing had arrived and now we jolly sailor men were kitted out in full battle dress complete with shirts, vests, pants, boots and socks, and forage cap. This meant goodbye to the Italian Navy whites, but they were to be put to good use in due course.

Out of all the chaos eventually came order. Each hut was to take its turn to act as council refuse removers, and to this end pits about a yard long by half a yard wide and two feet deep were dug outside each tenement. Into these pits were to be thrown empty tins (anything burnable being kept back for brewing up time). The said tins would then be collected in orderly fashion (Army) or disorderly fashion (Navy). These sessions would only come round about once every three months for each individual man, so there were many idle hours and days to wile away.

Something had to be done to alleviate the boredom of all this spare time, so a few of the "BEDOUIN's" crew got together, had a good look around for possibilities, and finally decided that the bare patch of baked hard earth which could laughingly be called a parade ground, had just the requirements for a quarter size football pitch, ideal for five a side games.

After consulting with the Camp R.S.M. and British C.O. the idea was put to the Camp Commandant. He agreed, so in no time whatever, a quarter size pitch appeared. The Italians supplied enough lengths of wood thick enough to take the strain of having bodies hitting them at high speed and soon two sets of goal posts were set up. Next, by virtue of scrounging, searching and indeed pinching lengths of string and rope, a pair of nets took shape and at every match were proudly and ceremoniously attached to the posts, and then removed for safe keeping at the end of the games played.

First of all there had to be a list of all those who wanted to play, and it was then suggested that there be inter-hut games, which could then be split into league type divisions, and that there should be inter-services games. The inter-service games were quite naturally the biggest crowd pullers, and in actual fact, everybody looked forward to watching, if not playing, to all the games. Finding a ball was not a problem, the Red Cross had sent sports gear to the camp which included several footballs, and football shirts and shorts.

What the Italians had not noticed about the siting of the pitch, was the simple fact that a whole bunch of power cables ran diagonally across the pitch, hanging with a decided dip in the part directly above the centre of the pitch. Now it requires little imagination to see what possibilities that opened up for the lads.

It first happened as dusk began darkening the evening. The game had nearly ended when someone, clearing the ball from his goal area, booted it high into the air. Chaos! It went straight into the middle of the collection of cables, and Lo and behold, there did come forth a lot of brilliant sparks, and all the camp lights failed. From that moment we knew we had a way to upset the Italian militia, and more especially the Fascistti Carabinierre. From then on, as games went on into the dusk, up would go the ball and out would go the lights. Of course, there were profuse apologies to the duty Italian officer, given with an innocent expression on the face that was bursting to roar out with laughter.

As winter drew nearer, it was decided to ask the Italians if they would mind us using a field, nicely grassed and next to the generator house, and turning it into a full sized pitch so that proper teams of eleven men could play. They agreed and set up a pitch, even providing proper goal posts. We were delighted, only there was a snag. Right in front of one goal, and a couple of yards from it stood a great big power line pole. As we said, typical bloody Ities!

There had been a hunt on for talent. The so-called dining and recreation hall had been, with the blessing of the Camp Commandant, turned into a theatre, complete with tiered seating so that one could either, depending on how near the front of the queue one was, have a seat in the front stalls, or at the back up in the gods. Those wanted were musicians, or in fact, would be musicians (they were ready to give lessons to improve your musical skills).

Anybody with acting experience was wanted, or any who had been in S.O.D.S. operas, had stage experience etc, etc. The Entertainments Committee had a full programme hatched out for the winter months when we would be better off in the theatre than moping in the huts. In the pipeline were such plays as 'The Man Who Came to Dinner', 'The Importance of being Earnest' and musical recitals such as the one I went to Schubert's Unfinished Symphony.

We were now getting to know some of the characters of the camp, Italians like the Fascisti Carabinierre we called 'Farmer Giles'. He was a bully boy, liked to use the butt of his carbine if he could, and a very brave soul only so long as his opponent was completely unarmed and up against a wall. Well, every bully meets his match (and fate) some day. (From this point I shall refer to the above types as just Carabinierre, as they were only the military variety. The real Carabinierre were and still are, the Police, and wear a blue uniform and tricorn hat, and their trousers have a broad red stripe down the outside of the legs).

A trait we found about the Italians was the fact that they would never commit themselves to a straight answer. We got the same answer each time we asked a serious questions such as "When can we expect the next shipment of Red Cross parcels?", asked at a time when there had been a hold-up at the Swiss/Italian border. Always the same word "domani" (tomorrow). You all know what happens to tomorrow!

The daily musters, the first at about 08.30 and the second at 17.30, were a cause of some innocent merriment, although the object of our merriment often irritated the Sergeanti-Majori in the charge of the count, and held up our activities for up to half and hour or more. Often the private accompanying the Sergeant-Major would be a complete ignoramus from the backwoods who, once he had reached ten on his fingers had to stop, screw his face up in concentration trying to remember what came next, and then had to start all over again. The count should have been simple, as we having double bunks, stood two at the foot of each set of bunks. Quite honestly what we saw convinced us that the Italian Army must be full of dull, dim witted, unintelligent illiterates. Only the N.C.O.'s showed any sign of sense, schooling and literacy.

A word about these bunks. They were made of wood, with one bunk above the other, held together by wooden pins or wedges. The actual bed part looked like an oversized seed tray, with wooden slats spaced about an inch or two apart along the length of the bottom. These were to take the strain of the mattress and accompanying person seeking well earned rest. The mattresses we had to stuff ourselves with straw, the more straw one could stuff in the mattress cover, the more comfortable the mattress would be. Ah well, we lived and learned. The pillow was likewise to be stuffed with straw, and we were actually given an extra blanket. The whole structure was very rickety, and it was frightening when the occupant of the top bunk climbed up into his bed after the bottom bunk occupant had turned in, because the whole structure swayed and creaked like a broken down barn in a tempest.

One aspect of camp life I have not touched yet is 'Brewing up'. There were no ready made stoves abounding in the camp, one had to provide one's own cooker. We found that the South Africans were adept at making things such as these, and we soon began to make our own. Tools required were (a) one pair of sharp scissors, (b) a mallet, usually made from the smaller branches from the wood we collected, and, (c) a sharp, fairly large nail, this used as a sort of centre punch. Material required were any medium to large tins (from Red Cross parcels).

The first crude cookers were in the form of an open fire. The tins collected for this were first cleaned, then the bottom was removed by means of a butterfly tin-opener, then the body of the tin cut across and the top and bottom edges trimmed off. Now the oblong piece of tin plate had to be hammered flat, and when the requisite number of tins had been dealt with thus, the task of fitting them all together started.

First the long edges of the plate had to be turned over so that one sheet fitted into the next and so on. This was the point where the nail came into use. After fitting two sheets together by the turned over edges, they were then flattened with the mallet, and firmly secured by popping all along the join using nail and mallet. Almost like riveting. When enough sheets had been fitted together, they were then bent into shape and the two ends joined and rivetted.

Next, holes were made to take the firebars, other sheets of tin turned over into a thick bar, and these were fitted. Cross bars were also fitted above the firebars for resting the dixie on, leaving plenty of space for loading in the wood required for the fire. All that was required now was to cut a hole for draughting the cooker and one was ready for the first home made brew.

From this first crude fireplace things progressed rapidly to much more stylish and elaborate stoves, even with double fireplaces and ovens. Ingenuity became the watchword. Seeing the work which came from the South African quarter, it was remarked one fine day that it wouldn't be surprising to see a Matilda tank appear from one of the South African areas.

Then one day there appeared a chap carrying a piece of board which appeared to have a firebox attached to it. Then, when he put if down, there could be seen something which vaguely resembled a foreshortened elephant's trunk. Then, surprise! The clever lad had invented a forced draught fire. The floppy bit was a bellows, made from a piece of old Service waterproof, carefully made into a tube and then attached to a round tin which had a hole in the bottom and which acted as a valve. The other end was attached to a tin, from which a tube led into the firebox. The operation was simple, lift the bellows up with the finger off hole, then finger on hole and push down. Result, one puff of blue smoke. The fuel he used turned out to be dead embers from the old crude fires, restarted by lighting a few bits of paper and/or cardboard. At first sight it looked as if there were Red Indians sending up smoke signals.

Soon, quite naturally, the single bellows became upgraded to the Mk. 2 double bellows type on which a small secondary bellows filled as the main bellows was depressed, and then collapsed as the main bellows was lifted, thus giving a continuous steady flow of air to the firebox.

Then, finally came the ultimate design, the fan type Mk. 1. The simplicity of the model was breathtaking. A length of board, upon which there was built a firebox which was fire-bricked (local wet clay), and attached to a banjo shaped structure in which revolved a four bladed fan, driven by a handle on a pulley wheel via a belt to the fan axle, the air being drawn in through the aperture where the axle protruded through the banjo, and the axle fitted into two side struts as support for it.

This became a success literally overnight, mainly because it was fast and needed only bits of wood, charred, or charcoal as fuel. Thus any unused fuel could be doused and used again. However, this was only a one speed blower, and before long there appeared more complicated versions (Mk.'s 1a, 1b, 2, 3, etc) all of which had some variation of the original. One such appeared with no less than three belts, which if used correctly, gave three speeds. At superburn all three were in operation, the arrangement of the gearing giving the same effect as the fifth gear on today's cars, high speed with less energy required.

When the first bellows appeared, there also appeared a South African with one of this type. He used to go around the brewer uppers and ask for embers. He very soon got the nickname of 'Embers' after his cry of "Embers, any embers to spare?".

The main thing which caused the most trouble was the utter boredom. From time to time an argument turned into a heated row as the boredom made each and every one of us highly irritable. These upsets soon blew over and friends became friends again within a matter of minutes, when seeing the complete folly of such behaviour, we returned to sanity once more. One thing united us all, detestation of the enemy.

We had, I suppose, been in the camp for about a couple of months when we were informed that the Red Cross had sent a shipment of books, and a library would be opened in a few days. We were asked to donate any books we received, after reading them of course, to the library so that the variety and scope of books could be improved. This proved to be a boon, once in operation, books could be taken out and read at leisure, thus limiting to a certain extent, angry outburst due to boredom.

Personally, I read quite a number of books during the following months, from the Zane Grey western to biographies, and indeed gathered a vast amount of further knowledge of a few of the Admirals of the past and their battles. In fact these biographies were more amusing in many ways than the fictional books that were meant to be funny. Well, truth is often stranger and funnier than fiction.

As winter drew ever nearer, some news filtered through on the grapevine about the general progress of the war. We heard that there had been a great push in the Western Desert, and gradually it became clear that not only was this about a push, but about a large scale rout of the Axis forces, ie. Rommel had received a huge pounding and was in full flight. No matter, that did not affect us in the least, we were too far from the scene of conflict for it to have any effect on how we were treated, fed, etc and more especially on our being released from captivity. Italy would have to surrender first for that to happen.

It must have been late October or early November. The weather had become rather cold, there being no sunshine, dull and overcast. Wood for brewing had become scarce, which did nothing to improve our spirits. Then suddenly the wind started to blow, getting fiercer by the minute. Everybody decided to get under cover in their respective huts, if they could, otherwise remain in the hut they had paid a visit to. Then, down the valley came a great roaring twister, a swirling high powered wind bent on causing destruction.

It hit the camp. The huts swayed in the force of the wind, and we watched the roof of our hut lifting and falling back again, waiting for it to disappear. Next, there was a terrific crash at the rear end of our hut. At first we didn't quite know what had happened, and then we saw the roof and part of the shattered side of the double decker hut that stood directly behind us. When we finally got outside, we found that the hut behind us was now a single decker, the top floor completely gone.

Now, the want for brewing wood became too strong to be ignored, so, seeing all that broken wood lying about where it had become wedged under huts, a great exodus took place, and hordes of men swooped on these broken remains of a hut. I do not say that we got all the wreckage, because the Italians came belting in to try salvaging what remained of the upper deck. I believe they managed to salve just a part of the roof and eaves.

Not long after this incident, we were given notice that our forces were not lying down on the job. We had the first air raid warning since arriving. That one was during the day, although we neither saw nor heard anything. However, that night we did hear things. The bombers flew over the camp in a northerly direction, and soon after the sound of their engines had faded away, we heard the far distant rumbling of explosions.

The following morning, looking in the general direction of Genoa, we could see a black pall of smoke rising over the hill tops. One wag, leaning out of the top floor window of a double decker hut close to the rear fence, looked at the smoke and then yelled down, "I see the Ities are keeping their home fires burning". The glare given him by the sentry who was close by should have burnt that wag to a cinder. Well in evidence too, were 'Farmer Giles' and his merry gang of spoilsports. There was nothing he could do about anything at all, thank the Lord.

The warmth of summer and early autumn having faded, we were now entitled to take a hot shower once per week. For this luxury we had to march, by one hut each time, to the infirmary, well guarded of course by at least two guards. This showering routine had to be stretched out over the whole week, probably to prevent the old infirmary boiler from being overworked.

Despite this, possibly precautionary measure, the dust, dirt, low diet standards and probably low morale feelings, all most likely, led to the outbreak of Scabies, of which very few avoided. I caught it, and it really meant a hot shower every day.

With the dark nights upon us, the very thought of a night at the theatre became a desire. The two dim lights in the hut were useless to even try to read by, or try to write by. I do not think I have mentioned earlier that once in the camp we were allowed one postcard per fortnight, and every other week alternating with the postcard a foolscap letter. The first letter home gave all the information not given by the pre-printed card sent via the Vatican. The Italians must have wondered how so many of us had relatives and friends in the Royal Marines. Anything to do with the Italian running of the camp, food facilities etc, were always followed by "and don't forget to tell Cousin (or whatever) George in the Marines". Funny how the Italian censors never twigged the code. Never heard of it I suppose.

Worse still, we could not brew up after dark. Not surprising really, they did not want us to attract too many stray British aircraft. There had also been a hold-up on Red Cross parcels, and there had been reports that some wagons had been forced open and a number of parcels stolen. This was put down to guerrilla groups in the north who were anti Mussolini and anti German, and who were making a nuisance of themselves.

Somewhere about or around this time we had the first case, and I believe the only one, of theft of food from another person's Red Cross parcel. The punishment for this, a most heinous crime, was the loss of the thief's own parcel for one week.

In the run up to Christmas, we were told by the British camp staff, that some of the ingredients of our daily vegetable soup were being withheld in order to produce a bumper pasta. So, for a few weeks, the ration of macaroni and spaghetti disappeared from our daily soup. Nevertheless, we were entitled to a 31 gramme ration of fresh meat, which one could seldom find out on the days it was put in. But one midday, after the soup had been dished out, and we were contemplating the astonishing amount of plant life there was in it, one fellow leapt to his feet all excited, a beaming grin on his face, and yelled "I've got it. Fresh meat." Everybody wanted to see this fresh meat he purported to have, and gathered round as he proudly displayed his catch, a big fat CATERPILLAR!

Our worry now became, what if the Christmas parcels were stopped or stolen? Would Geneva send out replacements on time? But all our worries were for nothing. The Red Cross personnel travelled with the train and the guards ensuring nothing was touched or tampered with, and duly delivered to the camps in good time.

We made the best of Christmas 1942. The pasta produced by the galley staff was a superb concoction, a really solid and filling meal and tasty. After filling ourselves with that, there was not much space for anything else. Luckily, personal cigarette parcels had arrived in bulk during the week before Christmas, so there was no shortage of smokes.

So 1942 passed and 1943 arrived. The winter weather being particularly depressing, cold, wet and, outside the huts, everywhere was a great slippery mud heap. Spirits were not helped very much by this, nor by the fact that leaks appeared in some parts of the huts. Very often the central gangway became blocked because beds had been moved to avoid them getting wet during rainstorms.

Then, with such low spirits under these conditions, as the weather turned ever so slightly warmer, the inevitable happened. Lice! When spirits are low, so the body is low to resistance against these parasites. Soon, when the sun put in an appearance it was warm enough to get outside, hundreds of the inmates could be seen with jackets, or trousers in their hands and a lighted cigarette being kept brightly alight as it was used to run it up and down the seams of the clothing burning out what lice and nits could be found. Within a short time however, a large boiler appeared in the camp, and hut by hut a programme of delousing took place.

With the coming of spring, we had hoped that things would improve. But no! First, Red Cross parcels began to dry up. Then we found our compulsory rations were on the blink, sometimes we got them, sometimes not. These small commodities, sugar, cheese, polony (a kind of sausage), each a ration of 31 grammes per day, which we used to receive once per week in bulk, were a valuable part of our diet. However, complaints to the Camp Commandant brought forth the answer that as soon as these items were received in the camp he would have them issued and all back rations would be given with the rations of the present week.

Italian cigarettes were also an issue and the Camp Commandant, really a man of his word, also issued back rations of those as well. It was under these circumstances that we found how honest and sincere the Big Man was. He was not loath to come into the camp himself and explain the situation, more especially in the case of Red Cross parcels.

There were no back issues of parcels unfortunately, but there did come some bulk issues of dried vegetables from Argentina. At the time we were able to spend some of our camp Lira on fresh vegetables in the canteen. I laughingly call it a 'canteen'. It just so happened that some of us purchased a few items on the day an issue of this bulk dried vegetables was made.

Well, of course, these dried vegetables were a source of innocent merriment, to say the least. One lad decided to have a go at cooking them. He put some in his dixie and filled same with water, remarking that an overnight soak would do them the world of good. After he was safely fast asleep, another chap, who had managed to find some onions, cut a fairly large cross section from the bottom of an onion and put it in the dixie with the dried vegetables, saying "That should shake him."

The following morning, up jumped the owner of the wet vegetables and then gave a shout of surprise. "Look at this mates, those dried vegetables seem to be a bit of alright." Then, removing the piece of onion which had blocked out sight entirely of the other occupants of the dixie, gave another shout, this time of anger. "What lousy bastard put this in here?" Then followed the howls of laughter with such comments as "Can't you take a joke then?" etc, after which he had to admit he had been caught out very simply, and joined in the laughter.

Those Argentine dried vegetables were about the worst things ever sent to us. There was no way we were ever going to be able to cook them. Soak them as much as you liked, they would not swell up into full sized pieces of potato, carrot, peas, turnip or swede, they remained stubbornly tiny solid pieces of uneatable tack.

Over the winter months, the shortage of brewing wood had resulted in some large depredations to the woodwork of both bunks and loft flooring, our ceiling. As regards the bunks, in most cases the struts supporting the mattress had been taken out, so that every other one was missing. This, of course, was where the fan type fire came in handy, because from one strut the embers produced lasted quite a long time. This, coupled to the fact that walks were no longer the norm, helped to keep the depredations to reasonable limits.

The warm spring weather brought another menace with it, bed bugs! These little parasites nearly drove us potty. It seemed that no matter what one could do to combat them, they found a way round it. in the end it resulted in us taking our mattresses and pillows outside with sheets, which had thoughtfully been provided by the Italians, but only after some sharp words from the Authorities in Geneva, and sleeping on the ground. This was the only way we could ensure getting a good nights sleep, provided we were not disturbed by an air raid or a sudden shower of rain.

At first the Carabinierre did not like it, especially Farmer Giles. However he had orders from high places to leave us alone, we would only be disturbed if there were any air raids. During the day all bedding had to be inside, which led to some discomfort.

The flies, another source of annoyance, were of many varieties, and some were literally blood-suckers. One would lie or sit on one's bunk with a sheet wound around like a shroud, hoping to keep the flies at bay. Then there would be a low drone which gradually rose to a high pitched whine, just like a dive bomber coming down, and there would be a thwack on the sheet, and if you were lucky the blighter missed hitting you, but if you were unlucky, it drew blood. I know that too well.

One day, an Italian officer came into the camp and took a stroll round and stopped to have a natter with several of the lads. They were asking him all kinds of questions, and then one of them asked him something about how the war was going. He stopped talking, half turned and dived his hand into his pistol holster. All around him stepped back in alarm, when with a smile on his face, he produced a pair of sunglasses and put them on. He was not carrying a pistol at all!

The 'canteen' had for a while been selling 'vino'. We were allowed to buy a litre of this fearful concoction, per person, and each and every time we decided to go to the canteen, if we wanted the awful stuff. Demand for the raw vino soon took a nose dive, but as it was now drawing toward the 15th June and the first anniversary of our sinking, it was decided that a celebration should be held. So, round to all the other huts went our representatives, buying up all the wine they could lay their hands on, ending up with buckets full of the stuff, it all being carefully covered and kept safe until the great day arrived.

I am sure the Italian authorities were not quite prepared for what did happen on 15th June 1943. Nor was the camp really. the start of proceedings were toasts for all kinds of things, with sincere acknowledgements to the members of the crew who had not come with us and were now lying in an unmarked grave far down in the depths of the Mediterranean Sea along with our ship.

After that start, drinking went on in real earnest, I fail to see how so much of that wine was drunk, I had a cup of it but then refused any more, it was like drinking strong vinegar. However, those who had drank plenty got into a very merry mood, and before long had gone out to the small square and with one Jock Gibbons acting the part of the Camp Commandant 'Hopalong', were doing their version of Italian squad drill. This really was taking the Mickey, a bit too far, and the authorities that be took exception to it and ordered the square be cleared and those horrible English escorted to their huts to cool off. Well, in came a couple of rather scared looking guards who were promptly, and without ceremony, chased out of the compound.

Well, that started it. Those guards went back and complained, and shortly after, a platoon of Farmer Giles' carabinierre arrived (just like the 7th Cavalry in those westerns) and proceeding to fix bayonets, advanced into the compound. The situation became tense, the sheer defiance confronting those Italians made them stop and think for several minutes, but then they advanced trying to look brave, and soon the revellers decided that discretion is the better part of valour, and all beat a hasty retreat and took cover in our huts. The outcome was a rather naughty, spiteful night on the Italian side, but a gleeful one on ours.

We had the guards in the hut all through the night, and woe betide anybody foolish enough to put his foot over the end of his bed, it was sure to be given a belt with a rifle butt. All of us, innocent and guilty, whether proved or not, were given a cells sentence, a week each if I remember rightly, but only a few ever did their time. After all, there was only one cell for the whole 4,000 in the camp, and, it appeared, a shortage of guards to look after that one cell. In any case, as it transpired, those cells were not to be of any use to anybody in the very near future.

By July 1943, everything seemed to be going wrong for us P.o.W.'s. Red Cross parcels were only getting through spasmodically, and in fact camp supplies were in a state of fluctuation, some days all there, other days extremely short. Wood for brewing up what tea or coffee we might have saved up had become so scarce as to be nonexistent. The huts were mainly held together by luck and faith, so much of the structure had been removed for firewood. Beds were down to the barest essentials to keep them looking like beds. My mattress was spread across a mere four slats.

Then, like a couple of pantomime fairies, came two Italian workmen carrying a large telegraph pole. The intention was that more power cables were required for the camp and extra lighting, and this pole was to carry some of those extra cables. Having placed the pole carefully down, the workmen sat upon it and had a few minutes rest and smoke. Then they made their fatal move, they got up and left the camp to fetch their tools.

Beady eyes had been watching the progress of the pole from the first moment it had appeared, and as soon as the workmen were out of sight, the pole was spirited away and was never seen again. the funny part now came. Back came the two men and, still nattering away to each other, strolled to where they thought they had left the pole. First, puzzlement spread across their faces. Looking round they were obviously not too certain that they were at the right spot. Another good look further still did not produce their pole. What to do? The perplexity on their faces was comical to behold.

There was only one thing to do, report a missing telegraph pole. So back to the gate they went. Some ten minutes later back came the workmen accompanied by several guards. Over to where the pole should have been. Another thorough search of the whole area, and another conference. The guards obviously thought the men had left the pole somewhere else and were making excuses for not being able to do the job. However, the N.C.O. in charge of the guards decided to make a search of the camp, if only to satisfy the workmen, but look as they may, not a sign of that pole was to be found. Not even a speck of sawdust which might point to it having been sawn up, not even a small splinter and certainly no signs of freshly chopped wood in any of the huts. The following morning though, there were many happy brewers uppers at work down on the brewing square. That mystery must remain a mystery, at least to the Italians. No action was ever taken against anybody in the camp either, no positive proof.

The war news, such as we heard, or could glean from crafty questioning of various guards, N.C.O.'s and Italian officers, was very good, at least for us, although the Allied forces were still far to the south. We were confident, though, that it would not be too long before we were freed.

Bad news came from the Red Cross parcel front. Even the Camp Commandant came personally to tell us that a whole train load of parcels had been hijacked soon after crossing into Italy, and that some Italian troops may have been involved in the robbery. Other reports showed that Italian civilians were responsible for thefts from these parcel trains. We were in a very tight situation as regards parcels, our parcel store being almost empty, although we were told that a train with a fortnights supply of parcels would be arriving within days. This did prove to be true, and we were stocked up again slightly.

CHAPTER SIX

Goodbye Italy. Hello Germany.

8th September 1943 had begun the same as every other day in Campo Concentramento P.G. 52. The same camp routine had been carried out, the same counts and musters in the huts, camp cleaning parties as usual, the unemployed strolling and talking or brewing tea or coffee on the many assorted kinds of home made stoves. In fact it was a perfectly normal day until evening fell.

News gleaned from the Italian newspapers had given everybody a hope of a quick release, a hope which ran high in many breasts. What was not generally realised was the distance yet to be covered by the Allied troops before they finally reached as far north as Genoa.

As yet the Allied troops had only got as far as Naples, and had yet to overcome the fierce resistance the Germans were to put up at Monte Cassino. A further year was to pass before the gates of Rome were to be opened to them.

The swift advance across Sicily, and then the rapid invasion of Italy was not lost on the prisoners in Camp 52. The hopelessness of the Italians was not lost on them either. Almost everybody expected daily to see some sign of British or American troops and it was only the very cautious that predicted that there was many a slip twix cup and lip. Those cautious ones pointed out that the Allies were still a long way away, and what of the hordes of Germans falling back to new defensive positions. Would they not do something about all these prisoners of war?

The main topics of conversation then were the chances of the Allied troops reaching them, and the more immediate and pressing problem of the acute shortage of food parcels. The parcel store was now devoid of food parcels, with the exception of a few medical food parcels.

To keep hungry minds off such thoughts, and to keep up the spirits in the camp, a whist drive had been arranged in the recreation hall for that night.

I had arranged to go with a chum of mine as partner, so soon after the evening muster and brew of tea, the pair of us wandered down to the hall. Before long the whist drive was in progress, and only the sound of the M.C. calling trumps for the round, and the low mutter of the players could be heard.

Around 20.00 we were startled by a sudden outburst of bangs and the whooshing of rockets being fired. Almost everybody got up to look out of the high windows and someone managed to catch a glimpse of fireworks being let off in the hills around the camp.

The comments made were typical of the day and the feelings. "Bloody Ities bastards, why must they make all that f****** noise?". Then back to the game in hand.

Within a few minutes however, there came another outburst of firework explosions, more prolonged this time, and just as prolonged were the exasperated remarks of the card players.

Then, as the whist drive was about to resume playing, a further interruption came, this time from one of our own men. Wildly excited, a figure burst into the hall and leapt on to a table near the door.

"Hey fellas! The war's over! The bloody Ities have jagged in!"

"Oh piss off!" "Get stuffed!" "Have you told the bleeding Ities the news yet, stupid?" "Do you mind removing that revolting body to the outside and shutting the door behind it?" "Sod off and let's get on with the game!" and many more suchlike replies, rude and otherwise, were hurled at the bringer of glad tidings. Nobody present believed a word that had been spoken, so many practical jokes in like vein had been played like that before. However, as the purveyor of good news leapt off the table and hared for the door, interest in the whist drive began to wane. What had just been told them, plus the fact that the Italians seemed to be celebrating something, planted a very tiny seed into the minds of those present, and in spite of the M.C. calling for the game to continue, little groups began to form and discussions started.

Doubt was not to be left in our minds very much longer, because within a few minutes the Senior British Medical Officer and the Camp R.S.M. strode in, and climbing on to a table, held up a hand for silence. Slowly the hubbub died away, and the Doctor spoke, quietly, but his words hit like the kick of a mule.

"Gentlemen, Italy is out of the war! News has just reached me that they surrendered unconditionally this morning. What you have heard outside are the civilians celebrating the end of the fighting against the Allies."

At this there came a terrific burst of cheering, and everyone began slapping his neighbour on the back and shaking hands with all those nearest, and faces that had hardly known a smile for months broke into broad beaming smiles. Again silence was called for, and when quiet was once again restored, the Doctor spoke again.

"Although it is true that the Italian soldiers are no longer our enemies, they still have the job of guarding this camp, and will continue to do so until relieved by Allied troops. There may be some nasty minded persons among the Italian populace, and it will be the job of the Italian soldiers to stop them harming you. I must ask you all therefore, not to attempt, however strongly you may feel about it, to leave the camp. Carry on as usual, our troops should be here before long. And now gentlemen - The King!"

It will take a lot to make me forget that moment. I cannot remember when I have heard the National Anthem sung with such heart. Another long burst of cheering followed, and as this died down the strains of 'Land of Hope and Glory' started, and as many others had joined those already in the hall, the singing of this well loved song rose to a crescendo, ringing out all over the camp, to be followed by another long bout of heartfelt cheering. Only smiling faces could be seen on this memorable night.

The lighter side of this momentous occasion came by way of the Italian sentry at the main gate. On hearing the news, he had promptly slung his rifle into his sentry box, thrown open the gate, and grabbing the nearest of the prisoners to the gate, had, full of excitement, performed an impromptu dance with him. Then, when he had gathered in a few more, he danced a wild and exuberant ring-a-ring o' roses, finishing by kissing each one on both cheeks.

Suddenly realising that he had a duty to perform, he warmly shook hands with the small gathering of prisoners, and shutting the gate went back to retrieve his rifle and resume his post again.

Food may have been in short supply, but that did not worry us any longer. On the strength of what we had been told, we dashed off to our huts, and despite the fairly late hour for such things, got out the brewing material, and whet our dixies of tea, with which we toasted the end of the war for the Italians, and toasted our rapid return to our homes and loved ones.

Even food put by for emergencies was dug out and consumed in the excitement and momentousness of the occasion. It was very late that night before finally snores could be heard from every hut, and the last reveller had dropped off to sleep, dreaming pleasant dreams of the morrow.

It was a very happy camp the following morning, the 9th September. There was no muster to interfere with our routine and although the camp cleaning parties carried out their usual jobs, nothing else in the way of work was done.

I was one of the many who were strolling up and down inside the perimeter wire that fateful morning, talking to one of my close chums. Our eyes were on the main road outside the camp most of the time, waiting and watching with growing impatience for the arrival of the Allied troops which we expected to see at any time now.

A little before 11.00 we were rewarded by the sight of several lorries drawing up opposite the main administrative quarters on the main road, and of seeing khaki clad figures clamber unhurriedly from them. These figures made their way toward the camp, and when we could see them a bit more clearly we could sense there was something wrong.

The khaki did not strike as being quite the right shade for British troops, if anything it was slightly darker. Then the way in which the equipment was slung did not ring a bell. Before the approaching soldiers had got halfway to the camp gates we realised what was wrong. They were not British or American, they were German!

The shock of the realisation struck us all motionless for a few moments, and then the paralysis left our limbs, and with one accord we all bolted for the corner of the camp farthest from the approaching omens of prolonged captivity.

Again we were doomed to disappointment, for standing there with his carbine raised menacingly, and threatening to shoot anyone who made an attempt to climb the wire, was the one Carabinierre we all hated, and, although we did not like to admit it, feared because of his utter ruthlessness, the one we knew as 'Farmer Giles'.

For the moment we stopped, not knowing quite what to do, but though the growl went up to scrag 'Farmer Giles' and stuff his carbine up his anal passage, the hesitation proved fatal. The Germans had moved extremely fast, and by now, moving round the camp in a pincer movement, had almost surrounded the camp, unceremoniously shoving the Italian soldiers out of the way, taking their rifles and then booting them on their way.

Naturally enough 'Farmer Giles' became the butt of many threats, most of them to take his life in the most slow and painful method. The peculiar part of it all was that we were to see him once more, but in entirely different circumstances, when our vengeful thoughts turned to gusts of laughter at his sorry plight.

The German troops that had taken over the camp turned out to be some Austrian conscripts, and a silent, almost unsmiling lot they turned out to be. Although we asked them many and varied questions, they refused to make any answers and only gave the briefest of smiles.

The routine of the camp was in no way interfered with, we were allowed to carry on as usual, although they did make a check count. No work was asked of us, which maybe was just as well, with the exception of getting in our rations.

We had a Polish lad in the camp, and his one fear was to be caught by the Germans so, during one of the ration collecting trip, he walked out and away. I doubt very much if the German ever caught up with him.

This first lot of German troops only stayed for 24 hours. The next day around noon they were relieved by another company, while the first lot continued to travel north, whether to Germany and leave or not is a matter for great conjecture.

By this time some of the stalwarts of the camp were getting very impatient and annoyed, so they assembled in the recreation hall, fully equipped with Red Cross boxes and digging implements and started a tunnel.

The idea seemed to be to dig their way out to the river bank, and then escape along it if possible. The Germans did not seem to be aware of what was going on, and took no notice, apparently.

Suddenly a whole gang of them descended on the ground between the perimeter wire at the back of the recreation hall and sowed anti-personnel mines deep, thick and fast. That put the damper on any further thoughts of tunnelling out that way, and there was no other way to get out now, except through the main gate or over the wire.

So the 10th and 11th September passed by quietly. On the 12th came the first move. The troops who had been guarding us for the past two days were moving off to Germany, and in the course of going, were taking some of us. Fortunately, or unfortunately as the case may be, I was in the first batch to go.

Those of us going had to pack our gear, and were then fell in on the main road outside the camp. The German troops then took up their positions and marched us off. Transport to Chiavari Station was to be Shank's pony after all.

The 14km march was full of light amusement, both for us and for the Germans. Several of the chaps with light loads stepped out of the ranks at every conceivable moment they thought they were not being observed and dived into hedges, down farm tracks and into open doorways, but the answer was always the same, the Germans just followed them and smilingly brought them back into the fold, with the shake of the head and an admonishing wag of the fingers. Never once did I see a weapon unslung or used as a threat by this company of German soldiers.

Eventually we reached Chiavari Station and there we were taken to the sidings and lined up by the side of a train of wagons, each wagon bearing the legend '40 MEN or 8 HORSES'. The outlook did not seem too good, forty men in one of those wagons was going to be a tight squeeze.

After a short while, we were sorted out into batches of forty, each batch being moved in position opposite the wagon to which it was detailed. Then from each batch of forty, a couple of men were detailed to go with the guard. These men were to fetch some Red Cross parcels, for the few that were left in the camp at the time of the Italian surrender had now been transported to Chiavari Station. Most of these parcels were medical parcels of food, sent originally to help the diet of those sick and in hospital, or otherwise in need of a special diet.

We finally received the parcels, which worked out at one parcel between eight men, very small solace to us, as we had little in the way of food with us. The Germans did allow us to collect as much water as we could safely carry in flasks, bowls or dixies. There was no knowing when we would get more water, and we did not intend to be left short.

Although the train was ready for us to embark in it, the Germans made no attempt to force us into it, rather they let us get all the fresh air and exercise we could. Even with this certain amount of freedom, we were very closely guarded, but that did not prevent active minds seeking for a way of escape, if not from the station, then from the train once it had got under way.

All too soon for us, we were ordered to embark. Sunset was not far away now, and we had guessed that the train would not move off until it had the cover of darkness. While we were waiting for the train to move, after we had embarked, the Germans left the doors of the wagons open, but guarded, and we saw the very sorry state the Italians had come to as regards rail travel and transport.

Like us, the Italians had to travel in goods wagons, each wagon having a back to back seat running along the length of the wagon, and for night travel, straw had been provided on the floors of each wagon. We were crowded and uncomfortable, but what must it have been like for those civilians, travelling in such a way, and with the doors of the wagons open all the time, especially for the women and children.

Finally, the doors were slammed to and locked from the outside. The train began to move, very slowly indeed, those of us who could, got to a point of vantage from where we could see what the countryside was like outside. If the train was going to crawl along as it was doing, then there might be a chance of getting out under cover of complete dark.

Inside my wagon there was already some activity. A hunt was on for any kind of weapon which might be of use to undo screws or chip at wood. A glance out of the ventilation grille at the top of the wagon soon dispelled any idea of getting out that way, a grinning German guard was looking right down on us from his perch in the brakeman's shelter, which is to be found on most of the old Continental goods stock.

An attempt was made on the screws securing the bottom ventilation grilles, but these proved abortive, several knives being ruined in the process.

The next attempt was on the floorboards. Here we had better luck, for apart from breaking one knife, we found that with a little bit of chipping we could move one of the boards.

Moving this board would give access to the others, and we hoped to have a great big hole in the bottom of the wagon before very long, and then with the utter blackness of the early night before the moon rose, we hoped to be able to drop through the hole and on to the track between the rails and let the train pass over us, vanishing off the track once the train was safely clear of us.

The proceeding was not without its risks, but we were quite willing to accept them. Anything was better than being carried off into further captivity again.

Luck was not to be with us unfortunately. After digging away for a very long time at the obstinate floorboard, working by the light of shaded matches and bits of lighted paper, it finally gave way and was lifted out. The board next to it was lifted, and then we made the awful discovery that there was a steel plate under the boards we had lifted.

Hurriedly other boards were lifted and those already removed were replaced, but always it was the same, steel plates under wooden boards. We had to be the unfortunate ones and be placed in a wagon that was made of steel throughout.

I cannot describe the despondency that came over us at that discovery. It drained us of all our heart. Miserably we settled down to sleep as best we could in the uncomfortable and crowded wagon. Not much sleep was possible, for the train seemed to know that we had been balked of our escape bid, and proceeded to waltz along the rails, jerking and rattling all the night long.

Dawn slowly came, watched by tired eyes through the grilles, but still the train jolted its unhurried way through Italy, having passed Genoa, Turin and Milan during the night watches.

With the coming of daylight the train stopped and the guards came to open the doors and let us out to attend the needs of nature. That was when they, as well as us, discovered that quite a large number had got away in just the manner in which we had planned during the night. One wagon was completely empty, and from another, over half had got away before the coming of light had put an end to activities. How many other wagons had men missing I do not know, but the figures of those gone was quite high.

The fact that so many prisoners had disappeared did not seem to worry the Germans. Probably they knew that the escapers only had a short time at their disposal in which to make their escape proper. Some of them did, in fact, last out in hiding for as long as six months before being picked up again by the Germans and brought back to Germany. (I found out on my arrival back in England that two of H.M.S. "BEDOUIN's" crew had made a 'Home Run'. They were among those who went missing on the first night of the journey.

The halt was very brief and shortly the train got under way once more and jolted across country to Verona. This town was reached about dusk and the train shunted into a siding.

Alongside our train was another train of open wagons filled with Italian soldiers. They also seemed to be captives and on their way to Germany. Also they did not seem to be very well guarded and I cannot see why they did not try to escape under cover of darkness.

Perhaps the Germans were not so worried about the Italians and that maybe why they were left in open trucks, whereas if it had been our mob of bandits, there would have been a train of empty wagons by the time daylight arrived.

During the night the train moved off again, but the following morning stopped once more at another wayside station. This time, when the wagon doors were opened, we got a view of a great vineyard. This was the very extensive grape growing and wine producing area of northern Italy we were in now.

A Feldwebel (German sergeant) came along and asked for our attention. He could speak very good English and seemed a cheerful sort of fellow.

"We are stopping here for a couple of hours," he said, "so if you will give me your parole not to try to escape, I will let three or four of you take a blanket and go into the vineyard and get as many bunches of grapes as you can carry. I have not many guards, but I will post some at the extreme edge of the vineyard. I will recall you by blowing a whistle."

The chance of getting something to eat, as well as the fact that the grapes would help to overcome, in some small way, the pangs of thirst we felt from time to time. We knew full well that we would not get any more rations until we were safely stowed away in a Stalag in Germany.

We accepted the terms thankfully and away went four out of the wagon. Some time later they reappeared lugging a bulging blanket that appeared ready to burst out its bottom any second. The loaded blanket was passed up into the wagon, and the large bunches of grapes shared out. There were two bunches each, and each bunch was the pick of the vineyard, weighing several pounds apiece.

The doors of each wagon were left open for some considerable time, even after the grape pickers returned although there was a German sentry standing close by. These Germans did not intend us to suffocate or see no sun while we were travelling.

After what seemed endless slow travel and pointless stopping and changing of locomotives, the day passed and night came upon us once more. More jolting and shunting after dark, and once more the fairly even motion of forward travel continued through the night. The morning of the 15th September found us at Bologna, where the train stopped clear of the station by a locomotive water tower, and we were allowed to climb out. There was an immediate rush for the water hydrant, first to get a quick wash, and secondly to fill up our water containers. Even in the rush we had time to notice that the Germans had carefully placed two lines of guards, one on the far side of the wagons and one line on the water tower side. There was to be no chance of escape at this time of the journey north.

In some cases the hatred of an enemy is ingrained into the children of a warring country, and that hatred will, and still, find some kind of an outlet, even though the two countries are nominally at peace. So it was at Bologna that while attending to our toilets, a small Italian boy wandered along the tracks and up to the train. He was chased away by the German guards, but in the manner of small boys, he persisted in coming back. Spotting us, he immediately burst forth into a torrent of abuse and invective against us. Naturally, he was told in his own language, and not very politely, to get out of our way and be quick about it. I think that our snapping back at him in his own language did more to make him run off rapidly than all the threats the Germans threw at him.

After an hour or so the train moved off again. Some languid progress followed, with here and there a spurt of high speed. We were rapidly getting into mountainous country, and from what we could see through the ventilation grilles, winding along valley after valley, ever climbing upwards.

That evening, just before dusk fell, we arrived at Brennero, just in Italy at the southern end of the Brenner Pass. Here the train stopped once more, and the Italian locomotive was detached and a German electric locomotive attached. As soon as the change of locomotives was completed, we moved off in to the Brenner Pass.

When morning came, and we felt like looking out of the grilles, we found that we were moving at a fast speed, through flat and rolling countryside, green after the sun-scorched appearance of the Italian countryside. A town came into sight and I noticed the legend 'Bank of München', then we ran through the station of München or Munich.

A short while later we ran through another small station, but the train was rapidly slowing down. A few minutes later, the train stopped altogether and the wagon doors were opened. We were on a siding not far from the town of Moosberg. This siding was on an embankment, and at the foot of which ran a road.

While waiting to disembark, a platoon of German soldiers came marching along the road, goose-stepping and singing one of those jerky marching songs for which the Wermacht were famous during the Second World War. Naturally enough, being British, we started to take the mickey out of this platoon of arrogant goose-stepping Germans. To us, this sight seemed like a scene out of one of the comedy films about the Third Reich that we had seen during our days of freedom.

With the disappearance of the marching column, we received orders to disembark. We were allowed to attend to our urgent needs of nature before being fell in on the road, formed up in a column of five deep and marched off.

Some ten minutes later the watch towers of a Stalag appeared in view, then the surrounding fences of barbed wire, and finally the Main Gate. We were halted at the gate while the Officer of the guard made a call at the Stalag Guardhouse. The gates were opened and in we marched, very reluctantly I might add.

Once inside the gates, they closed with a definite final thump, and our guards of the journey were replaced by guards of the Stalag company. We were halted again not far from the Main Gate and from a compound on our left came calls to us in Trans-Atlantic drawling tones. Here then were some of the American prisoners. We exchanged what news we could while waiting, and in all too short a time we were taken to a compound which had but recently been evacuated by Greeks.

Thus, at about mid-morning on 16th September 1943, we became finally and irrevocably, prisoners of the Wermacht, and non-paying guests of the Third Reich in their luxurious home from home hostel, better known as Stalag 7A.

CHAPTER SEVEN

Stalag 7A

Our new home did not at first seem much better than the squalid housing estates of the Italians, which had been hurriedly erected without much thought for the future tenants and non-paying guests of Il Duce. One thing we soon discovered was that these German built country houses were far better lighted than the Italian version and also did contain to some extent all the mod cons in the fact that there was a proper wash place with hot and cold water, and the latrines were made on a style to which we were accustomed to use in the British Isles, and they flushed.

How different to Italy, where when one required to pass motion, one had to squat over a hole between two slabs of slate, the trough below occasionally being flushed through, the exit from the trough being through a hole in the river bank, where all excreta found its way down to the river. No privacy here and what an awful stench all the time.

Here in Germany there was privacy such as one knew at home, where we could sit back in comfort and flush when finished, thus leaving no vile stench hanging about in the toilet area.

We soon sorted ourselves out into little groups and set out personal belongings upon the beds of our choice. In no time at all, so it seemed, a midday meal of potato soup and boiled potatoes appeared. This was for us a luxury indeed. Better still was to come, because soon afterwards there appeared on the scene a good ration of German sausage.

This german sausage gave rise to a peculiar incident. I had teamed up with the Wardroom Chef, one Ernie Lander, and having received our ration of sausage, then decided it would taste better if fried. So, proceeding to the space between our manor and the one next door, found enough fuel to build a fire and proceeded to cook our sausage ration. One side of the thick slice of banger looked as if it were cooked so we decided to turn it over. As Ernie stuck his fork into the meat there came a noise like a dachshund yelping. We both looked at each other and simultaneously, being quite startled, said in disbelief "It barked!"

However, before this, having settled the problem of our sleeping billets, we wandered outside for a breath of fresh air. I noticed a commotion at the gate of a compound some distance away, across a patch of ground that had not yet been used for building huts. A tall, commanding figure seemed to be having a rather heated argument with the guard at the gate, and backed by a press of other figures, seemed to be getting the better of it. The guard gave way finally, and the figure, somewhat familiar, followed by the others strode towards our compound.

When he was halfway across I and some of the others gave a shout of recognition. It was our Captain, Commander Scurfield, and most of our surviving officers striding towards us. We moved to the gate to welcome him.

After enquiring how many of us had arrived, he then asked when we had last seen a Red Cross parcel. He was most surprised when we told him of our plight, and immediately ordered an issue to us from the Officers stock which had been brought up from Italy.

As was to be expected, there was some opposition from the Army officers who had come up with him, but he happened to be the Senior British Officer in the Stalag, so he had his own way and in the early part of the afternoon, a supply of parcels arrived for us, one parcel between two men.

Commander Scurfield paid us a visit each day we were at Stalag 7A, making sure we had everything we required if it were possible to get it. His visits, and the casual and familiar way in which he spoke to, and with us Naval Personnel caused some amazement among the Army types. So far, they had not received a single visit from any of their officers, even to see if anybody present was from that Officer's old unit. Yes, even the soldiers came to look forward to our Captain's visits, for he spoke to them just as much as he conversed to us Royal Navy types.

We were not due to stay very long in Stalag 7A, but the few days we were there provided us with plenty to talk about and think over long after we had left.

Our compound was placed next to that of some Russians. These Russians were always on the lookout for a stray titbit from us, such as bread. The German Army bread took some stomaching at first, being so different from the Italian bread. It was black, heavy and had a very sour taste.

It was about a couple of days after our arrival that several of us happened to meet up with a Russian Officer strutting about by himself. As he could speak very good English, a conversation started.

The question arose about the Russians in the compound next to ours, and whether they belonged to the Red Army. The fact that we seemed to involve him and the Red Army with the sorry looking Russians next to us aroused his indignation. Drawing himself up, he exploded.

"I" he announced, pounding his chest with a clenched fist, "I am the Red Army. Those" waving a disdainful hand toward the Russian compound, "are serfs, peasants, slaves. They are not the Red Army. They are nothing. Why", glaring round at us, "the Red Army has not yet been used. When it is, nothing will stop it."

In the Russian compound, the main concern was food and this concern gave rise to the first of the incidents to take place during our stay in Stalag 7A. The start of this incident was some days before we arrived, but we saw the end of it.

Apparently one of the Russians had become very ill and eventually died. His companions were not going to be deprived of the extra food ration, so they concealed the fact that there was a dead man among them. For several days, at the times for musters, they had calmly announced to the German soldiers doing the musters that their comrade was sick. Then came the day when a suspicious German soldier did the counting and demanded that the sick man sit or stand up, and on receiving no reply, threw back the blankets and disclosed the dead man. Retribution followed swiftly for those Russians involved.

The second incident came about through the habit of the Germans of letting loose Alsatian guard dogs in the double barbed wire fences around the perimeter and also in the compounds, one of which just happened to be the Russian compound.

These dogs were let loose after dark as a deterrent to an escape effort and also to cut down the number of sentries required on the inside of the wire as well as those patrolling the outside.

On the first night of the occurrences, the dog was let into the Russian compound as usual and left to prowl around until it was retrieved the following morning by its handler. The only trouble was, in the morning there was no dog to retrieve, it had disappeared without trace. Despite the most thorough search by the Germans, not a sign of it could be found, nor any trace as to how it may have got out of the compound, if it had been so inclined.

On the second night a pair of dogs were let loose in the Russian compound. They too disappeared without trace. The Germans were by now well and truly baffled. They just had to find the answer to this mystery.

Two more dogs were loosed into the compound during the third night and a little later the dog handler slipped in as well. His job was to solve the mystery of the vanishing dogs and he was to roam all night until something happened to give him a clue. Unfortunately for the Germans, both dogs and handler vanished during the night, no trace ever being found of any article of uniform or other clothing, or of the dogs and their equipment. The Germans had to give up in despair and henceforth, neither dogs nor sentry were sent into the Russian compound after dark.

As it happened, we were only to stay at Stalag 7A for five days, but during those five days we had one official issue of Red Cross food parcels and three unofficial issues, one of which came from the Americans. This extra food was warmly welcomed by all, for we had been living on 'pani-aqua' (bread and water), very little bread and watery soup for several weeks before being brought into Germany. Food parcels had failed to arrive in Italy, although they were piling up on the Swiss border, because of the chaotic conditions on the Italian State Railways.

During the evening of 20th September we received orders to be ready to move in the morning. Early on the morning of 21st September we were mustered at the main gate and issued with a few tins of food from Red Cross parcels. This food was to last us during our coming journey. How long this would take we had no idea.

After receiving the food issue, we were marched to the same sidings from which we had detrained on our arrival here a little less than a week previously. Here we entrained again and, as before, were piled forty to a wagon. However, there was one refinement over our former journey, each wagon was fitted with an 'Elsan' chemical latrine. This meant we would not have much chance to get out of the train for a leg stretch during the journey and also pointed to a rather short trip.

How wrong was the speculation that this would only be a short incarceration in these wagons. The journey took seven days. In actual length, I suppose the mileage for the journey would be in the region of 600 miles, say from London to Glasgow and half way back (going via Plymouth and Aberdeen), or should I say that it seemed that distance and that way round. In no way can this journey be classed as express or even slow goods, it was more like a misguided mystery tour with a driver who didn't know the way.

The train wound its tedious way through such places as Leipzig, Nürnberg, Dresden, Chemnitz and many other such places and towns we failed to catch the names of, spending hours standing in sidings and often waiting in main line stations, parked on one of the spare coach storage tracks. The waits at the major stations were for the guards to get meals, which were laid on for them at these stations. Coffee was also provided for us from time to time as we slowly progressed, but these were the only times the doors of the wagons were ever opened during the whole time we were on that train.

Eventually, in the late afternoon, the train drew to a grinding halt at the little wayside station of Lamsdorf in Upper Silesia (Oberschlesia). Here we detrained, stiff and sore, aching in every limb. It took an effort to get our belongings from the train, cramped muscles refused to obey our wills for a time.

It was a typically fine sunny later summers day, and once we started marching, the sweat soon started to pour from our bodies. It took quite an effort to get going, but once on the move, tired as we felt, the cramped feeling soon wore off.

About twenty minutes marching, by which time I was wondering just how much further these heathen Germans were going to march us, brought us in sight of the camp. This was Stalag 8B (one of the biggest P.o.W. camps).

We marched in through the gates and some distance through the camp before we were ordered into an empty compound. We had been counted as we came in through the gate, but now we were warned not to leave this compound until after the evening 'Apell' (roll call), after which we could wander about the camp, with certain restrictions, until lights out sounded.

Settling on to beds and sorting out our possessions took most of our time that evening, and after the evening 'Apell', most of us were too tired to do more than turn in and sleep. Thus really began our long incarceration in Germany and some of us who arrived that day were to find graves on German soil.

CHAPTER EIGHT

A short stay in Stalag 8B

The day after our arrival at Stalag 8B we had to attend our first German interrogation. This proved to be most interesting and in a way amusing, due mainly to the methods used by the Germans.

The interrogation was carried out by girls, most attractive some of them too, and I can only assume that the Germans thought that once we were confronted by attractive women, we would give away things we should not have done. However, all they got from us was our names, numbers and ship, apart from a variety of civilian jobs which most of us had never known in our lives.

During the walk to and from the interrogation rooms, we had the chance to see some of the Canadian soldiers who were captured at Dieppe shuffling round their exercise area, all of them shackled and handcuffed with their hands behind their backs. We were rather hurriedly moved away from there, but several times afterwards we took the opportunity, when it came, to keep an eye on these men and if possible have a word with them.

It was on this first full day in Stalag 8B that we came into contact with the Camp Commandant. Contrary to expectations, he was not an Army officer, but a full-blown Captain of the Deutches Kriegsmarine (German War Navy). As, by the rules and regulations, we were under obligation to salute all officers, whether our own Navy, Army or Air Force, or whether they were officers of the enemy, we saluted the Commandant and, to our surprise, he acknowledge the salute with the Imperial salute and not the Nazi clenched fist arm shake that we had come to take for granted that all German officers would use. In all his meetings with Allied P.o.W.'s he never once gave the Nazi salute, it was always the Imperial salute and consequently he was respected for it.

We soon got into the routine of the camp and found it quite simple and not much to worry about. We could wander about the camp much as we pleased most of the day, and there were variety shows to see in the evenings if we so desired. These shows were put on by members of the camp and many were the would be actors who wished to try their luck in front of the footlights.

About the only place in the camp barred to us was the R.A.F. compound. The repatriation compound could be visited if we so desired, for in there were all manner of cases, from the totally disabled to the totally blind, reminders of the folly and futility of war. Most of these men needed the companionship of a person from other compounds who was sound of limb and wind and mind, it did a great deal to boost their morale and to help them to forget their own disability.

Things could not go on for ever like this though, some time some of us would have to leave. The Germans were not slow in finding jobs for us new blood. We could not live in luxury? for ever.

I suppose we were lucky in one way. We, as servicemen, were normally a bunch of non-go'ists when it came to church. One of our Engine Room branch members happened to be a Salvation Army member and through him we held our own prayer and hymn singing service in our hut. Much as he had been ribbed about being a church goer, we all gathered round him when he suggested holding a service.

After the first week had gone by, the draft chits began to pour in. First came the list of names for work in the sugar beet factories. Then came a list of names for work on the railways and in stone quarries. Then I got my job.

A list came in for work in Stamlager E51. My name was on it, as well as the names of eleven others of my shipmates. Instantly we all started to make enquiries about this job, where it was etc.

I can remember some of the remarks passed. "Here mate, you've been out at a working camp, so what's this E51 like?"

"E51! Blimey mate, you've got a right place you have. It's a bloody coal mine you're going to. Proper bastard of a place from what I've heard."

"You've got E51? Yes, I know the place, worked there myself once, before I got a right good kranker and got sent back here. I wouldn't like to be you blokes. I pity you. They're a gang of perishing slave drivers there."

"Where is it? Out in the wilds. Honest it is, somewhere on the Polish border as far as I know. There's a town called Glywitz not far away from it. Anyway, you can keep that camp chum."

"Yes chum, E51's a coal mine alright. I was in a camp not far from there. You have to be discharged dead to get away from that place."

Things did not look so bright for the hundred or so of us who had been detailed for Arbietslager E51. We twelve matelots among this bunch took a very dim view of it all. However, a matelot cannot be put down for long, as was soon to be proved.

Thus, ten days after our arrival in Stalag 8B, those of us who were detailed for Stamlager E51 found ourselves being marched from the Stalag to Lamsdorf railway station and once again stowed in wagons, forty to a wagon.

The journey this time only took us until the following morning, when we detrained at a siding outside Klausberg railway station. From here we were marched into and through the town and on to the camp, which was just outside the town and about half a mile from the mine in which we were to work.

Our arrival in the camp was the signal for news from the outside world, how the war was going, where had we come from etc. We gathered that our arrival was very welcome, we were new blood and new faces, but we must conform to the old stagers ideas. That idea did not suit us in the least, we were determined to make things as difficult as possible for the Germans.

CHAPTER NINE

The Working Camp. Arbietslager E51

Before anybody was put to work there were certain formalities to be dealt with. For a start there was a medical examination to go through. This was not much, but during it, one because he wore spectacles, another because of old wounds, and a couple more on some other medical grounds, and all matelots, were passed unfit for work in the mines. That was a good start.

Then followed the X-Rays and a further interrogation. The idea of this interrogation seemed to be to find out what kind of work we had been engaged in before joining the Forces, or the kind of work we had been engaged in during our time in the Forces. Needless to say, the Germans once again got a variety of mythical jobs thrown at them and they were left to sort it out the best way they could.

We were shown some empty rooms in the long huts at the end of the camp and Hut 20 became the quarters of us eight matelots with two South Africans and a mix of British 8th Army men from several different regiments, bringing the total in the hut to eighteen.

The first working day, a Monday, I had the morning shift from 06.00 until 14.00. This meant rising at 04.00, mustering at 05.00 and marching from the camp to the mine, where we had to change into the marked civilian mining kit with which we had been issued.

The permanent overseer, or stieger as he was called in German, was named Fuchs which translated means 'Fox'. he proved to be a very big man, standing about 6'4" tall and broad in proportion. One thing we found about him was absolute fairness, something not expected from a member of the Nazi party, of which he was a local bigshot.

It was very amusing listening to him trying to wrap his tongue round some of our names, particularly Brown, which he constantly pronounced as 'Broven'.

Although we all had P.o.W. numbers, we were also given a working number at the mine and had to collect a brass tally with this number on it each time we went to work and hand it in at the pithead on the completion of the shift. These brass tallies were the only check the Germans really had that everyone of us was out of the mine when we should have been. In the case of accident, the tallies were checked at the pithead as they were collected from the workers as they reached the surface. Any missing tallies could then be put down to somebody left below or trapped and rescue organisations could then go into action, while it was known on the surface who was missing.

The first frightening experience to the uninitiated is the rapid drop down the shaft made by the cage. These cages in the German mines are four deckers and miners entered them from two decks or levels at the pithead. With men in the cages the speed of descent or ascent is about 30mph, but with wagons, speed is around 45 to 50mph. Naturally, as the cage is suspended on a steel wire rope, when stopping at the required level below ground, the cage bobs up and down for a few seconds due to the inbuilt elasticity of the cable.

Ascending can be just as alarming, especially if one had to travel with the coal, as I did once, for the inertia which one has to overcome is startling. At first there is the feeling of being pushed into the deck of the cage, but more scaring is when the deceleration on nearing the top commences. then one feels as if the deck has started to drop away from under one's feet and it is a great relief to see the girders of the pithead come into view and realise that the direction of travel is still up. One eventually gets used to this.

Perhaps I was lucky to begin work under the care of the miner I did. He was 33 years old at the time and had worked in the mines from the time he left school. I met very few others who were as experienced as he was, or as careful and considerate. It was he who started me on the road to learning German. This he did by pointing out something, then giving me its German name and asking me to give its English name.

From such small beginnings I had, by the time I left Germany, learnt sufficient German to hold quite an intelligent conversation with any German.

That first day was sheer agony, not only for me, but for all the others who had come up from Italy. None of us had done a days work in Italy, with the exception of camp chores and we had grown soft and flabby. The effort of using a shovel bent backs and blistered hands. Muscles none of us realised we owned came out of hiding and added their throbbing to the agony of blisters and backache.

Then there was the stifling atmosphere of the workings, the smoke from the shot firings to fill our lungs and make them smart and cause our eyes to water and redden. The sensation, also, of being closed in, the unaccustomed creaks and groans of the timber props and the sudden pops in the coal face as a piece of coal would fly out under the enormous pressure above it.

As I have said, the miner I was with was most considerate and he let me rest quite a lot, doing the lions share of the work himself. Some of the others were not as fortunate.

One instance is that of one of "BEDOUIN's" signalmen, a lad named Curtis, an H.O. rating I shall from now on refer to as 'Bunts'. He was put to work with a fat useless slob of a German miner who, it turned out, was a hopeless case when it came to mining. This German was quickly nicknamed 'The Pig', mainly from the fact that he looked like one and acted like one. He was completely devoid of manners and was an arrogant bully. He was on top, or so he thought, and he meant us all to know it.

The fun started very early in the shift when Bunts stopped for a rest. Pig bellowed at Bunts to get cracking and stop loafing, to which Bunts told him in English to go and get stuffed. This back answer from a P.o.W. infuriated the Pig, it had never happened to him before, so he picked up a lump of coal and threw it at Bunts. To the Pig's surprise, a lump of coal came flying back at him, followed by a long string of oaths in English which traced his family tree from the apes to modern times.

The next move of the Pig was to threaten Bunts with a pick-axe. Not to be outdone, Bunts picked up his shovel and moved menacingly toward the Pig, yelling in English that one false move on the part of the Pig would result in one less German in the world. So it was when we packed up to go to the shaft, but the Pig just could not leave it at that. He thought that surrounded by his own kind he would be safe from any interference on the part of other P.o.W.'s. Once again he was out of luck. Although he stormed and raved like a madman he got nowhere fast and then he did a very foolish thing, he completely lost his temper and pulled out a flick knife, making a move as if to stab Bunts.

That move was enough for us in the vicinity. With one accord we turned on the Pig and he found himself glaring into distinctly hostile faces, murder written into each one. Luckily for him, he decided that discretion was the better part of valour and cooled off and no further trouble was had from that day.

The hot shower in the pithead baths helped to take some of the aches and pains from our bodies, but what we really needed now was a long sleep to relax and partly overcome the throbbing of long unused muscles. The only trouble was that we still had to attend evening Apell and that meant standing out on the parade ground for as long as it took the German soldiery to get the correct numbers and that might mean five or fifty minutes, perhaps longer.

The days slowly passed and our muscles rapidly became accustomed to the work, our bodies lost their flabbiness. Much of this may have been due to the German rations, which were much more than we had been used to in Italy. As the days passed, the Pig, given each day different P.o.W.'s tried to keep up his bullying, but only succeeded in making himself look more of a fool, both in our eyes and in the eyes of his fellow Germans.

The Germans expected to get more work out of us new hands, that was obvious, but they were in for a shock. We were up to all kinds of tricks to stop doing any work, from faking illness to downright sabotage.

Naturally we were paid for working, in lagermarks, which could only be used in the camp itself. What we earned went to help pay for issues of French cigarettes and occasionally the odd razor blade.

When we first arrived at this camp, all the matelots got themselves together in one room. Each room held 20 men or was supposed to, although in the room I was in there were seldom more than 18 at any time. After the initial sort out there only remained just 8 matelots, so the other members of the room were a couple of South Africans we knew well and the others were from the 8th Army and a mixture from the U.K. all of them good friends of us matelots.

There was a Dramatic Society in the camp and they welcomed us new faces, simply because some had acted in plays and sketches in Italy. Christmas being near, a pantomime had to be produced and this was where the new blood came into its own.

Christmas came and went and 1944 arrived. We had by now settled into the camp routine. The routine was not quite what the Germans had laid down for us, but rather a routine of our own. On the surface we were doing exactly what the Germans wanted, that is conforming to camp rules and working hard, giving no trouble whilst working. Actually, we were up to all kinds of mischief.

The first the Germans knew was when the Swiss delegates from the International Red Cross arrived to look round the camp. Much as the Germans tried to keep us away from the delegates, they could not. We had our say. We complained bitterly that we were doing war work and that was against the Geneva Convention.

Our complaint went through, but as expected it was ignored by the German High Command. We carried on working. Now that the High Command had ignored the International Red Cross ruling, we could begin to act more fully.

I have stated earlier that Steiger Fuchs was a very fair man. This was proved not long after the episode of the Pig. One of our young soldiers named Gerry was put to work with another of those nasty minded bully-boy Germans. During the course of the shift, an argument broke out between Gerry and his Hun boss, which resulted in the German taking Gerry to see Steiger Fuchs. When asked what was wrong, the Hun stated that Gerry had hit him. Asking Gerry what went on, he was told that the German had hit him. Steiger Fuchs then asked Gerry what he had done and Gerry replied that he had walloped the German back. Result, Steiger told German to get back to work and not to be such a cry baby.

From now on, mysterious things began to happen. We had found a certain way of reducing production without calling attention to ourselves.

All the machinery underground was electrical. The jig-pans were driven by electric motors, the bearings of which were lubricated by means of slip rings running in an oil bath. It was a simple job to slip a couple of handfuls of powdered coal dust into the oil bath when nobody was looking, preferably at the beginning of the shift. After an hour or so of running, the coal dust would work into the bearing, stop the oil from doing its job and the motor would seize up and burn out. That meant replacing the motor, a job that required at least two hours to perform, so production in that particular bit of the section was brought to a standstill.

In some cases, the stoppage of a jig-pan meant a complete stoppage of work throughout the section.

Then there were the endless conveyor belts. Once these were stretched beyond a certain critical length, they were the target for us P.o.W.'s. It had been found that a very heavy weight, if let fall on a belt from a fair height or distance, would part the belt. The object now was to find a sufficiently large mass of coal, and let it drop suddenly on the belt, when there would be a groan, then a ripping sound as the belt first stopped and then tore. Once again this would cause a hold up of two or three hours.

The Germans tried to get round these hold ups by exercising the right of an extra hours work to make up for lost production. Many times the words 'Eine stunde langer' (one hour longer) were spoken by the overseer. Just as many times, we P.o.W.'s either refused or, in most cases, just sat out the extra hour. One more hour down below made no difference to us in any case.

In the spring misfortune struck us matelots. Lofty Scoltock, a sparker, had an iron pipe fall on his back, resulting in a chipped bone in the spine. He was sent back to the main Stalag after a short time in hospital. Stalag 8B had by now become Stalag 344 and was the main camp for those awaiting repatriation and those too ill to work.

About this time, one of the longer serving residents in our camp stated that he was going to get out of the camp and get sent back to Stalag 344. "How?" he was asked. Tapping the side of his nose he quoth "Wait and see". For several weeks nothing appeared to be happening to make his boast come true. Then he started a change of character, appearing with staring eyes, muttering to himself, and generally appearing to go round the bend. He became so bad that even the guards kept well out of his way when they had him in the shift being escorted to the pithead. Nobody wanted to know him down below either.

Finally the Germans became so scared of him that they sent him to the local German Army Headshrinker. Back came the verdict in double quick time. "The lad's gone off his rocker! We will arrange for his quick removal to Stalag 344." Just about everybody in the camp were convinced that the lad had gone potty. Then came the day for him to leave for Stalag 344. He came out of his hut carrying what little luggage he owned (not much, same as the rest of us), looked at the assembled send off party, nearly all those not at work down the black hole, winked at us and quietly said "I told you I was going to get back into 344."

As had happened in Italy, as the spring weather gradually warmed up after the snow had melted, so came the appearance of bed bugs. At first nobody thought very much about it, but by Easter things were getting serious. Complaints were made about these pests, but without much notice being taken by the appropriate authority, namely the German Camp Commander.

After a while we were told to get hold of some creosote and stand the bed legs in it. Somehow we did get a little creosote, but it seemed to make very little difference. In fact things got worse. Beds were moved away from the walls, but that made not the slightest difference.

Then came the amazing discovery that these particular bugs did not come from out of the woodwork as they had in Italy, but were firmly ensconced in the straw of our mattresses and pillows. The question then became "How do we get over this?" The Germans showed no sign of sympathy with our plight, so we decided that drastic action was needed.

It must be remembered that the above events were happening in every hut in the British part of the camp. (We gathered that the Russian part of the camp was something akin to the old Newgate Gaol in its 18th Century heyday). So with our M.O. firmly on our side and backing whatever action we decided upon, we all took our mattresses and pillows off our beds and piled them in a heap out on the parade square. The Germans were quite forcibly told that if nothing was done about the bug situation immediately, the bedding would be burned.

That ultimatum had little more effect on the Germans than a raised eyebrow. It was hard at first to get any sleep lying on just bare boards, but we made the most of it. Just the same, the little pests seemed to be on the attack just the same as usual. As one wag in our hut remarked the following morning "You just can't beat the buggers can you? They are sending in their airborne troops now", this last being a reference to the fact that some had fallen on the beds during the night.

Thereafter we made the best of a bad job, but finally managed to get reasonably comfortable for the rest of our unwanted stay in this 'Holiday Camp'. Also we finally beat the bug menace and were happier for that small blessing.

So far Silesia had been fairly free from Allied air raids, but with the coming of spring and better weather, over came the bombers. At first everybody was hustled into the air raid shelters around the camp, but as time went on we refused to enter them, so the Germans made no attempt to try to force us into them.

It was a grand sight for us to see the tight mass of gleaming silver specks high in the sky and to watch them as they made their run up to the target, usually the chemical works and oil refinery in the

Oppeln area. The rumbling of the explosions reached us far from it as we all were.

The Allies were stepping up their attacks to a pitch never thought possible by the Germans. As fast as factories, refineries and the railways were brought back into operation, so the bombers came back and laid them waste again. The effect on the Germans was terrific. The arrogance began to fade and fear took its place. Morale began to go.

The Germans thought to get over this by working three Sundays out of four. This meant only one day off per month, but where the Germans began to crack under the strain, we P.o.W.'s seemed to thrive on it.

More and more were the Germans getting thrown at them by us that they were a beaten nation and might as well give in. But no! They wanted coal, coal and still more coal in order to win the war. Posters went up all over the mine. Overseers tried their best to get more work from us, but we continued in our own sweet way doing less and less, creating as much disorder as we could without being caught at it.

In the early summer there came to the camp a batch of P.o.W/'s from the area that had been heavily bombed of late. Some of these had been put to work clearing wrecked German aircraft from one of the airfields near where the bombing had taken place. They brought with them a complete short wave radio receiver which they had 'liberated' from a wrecked Messerschmidt fighter plane, broken down and concealed about them, and smuggled into the camp. This was to become our secret radio and from it we were to get all the news from the B.B.C.

It so happened that when D-Day dawned, I was on night shift. For some reason I could not sleep and about 15.00 I was lying awake on my bunk when in dashed one of the room inmates bursting with news.

"It's happened. Our troops have invaded France!"

Instantly everybody was awake. This indeed was good news. The end for the Germans could not be far off now. All of us expected to be home by Christmas at the very latest. Which just shows what wishful thinking can do.

A little later a full bulletin was sent round, but we were all strictly warned not to mention a word of the invasion, let the Germans tell us themselves. If the Germans found out that we knew of the invasion, they would certainly hit on the fact that we had a radio of some kind.

That night was most amusing for me. I was cornered at least half a dozen times and the Germans would look fearfully all around to make sure there were no Gestapo bogeymen nor another soul within miles of them and then whisper "Englander, das invasoren kommpt. Britisher und American soldarten komm schnell!" (Englishman, the invasion has come. British and American troops are coming fast).

All of these had been listening to the B.B.C.'s Overseas Broadcast in German, which was forbidden by the Nazi's under threat of severe punishment. German news broadcasts were so filled with propaganda that the B.B.C. was listened to in order to pick the truth from the lies.

Just as surely, the German propaganda machine went into top gear and overdrive. In order to throw the invaders back into the sea, the miners had to produce twice as much coal and then double it again, etc etc. To protect the Fatherland they must do without this and that. With the redoubled efforts of the workers everywhere, the danger to the Fatherland could be averted. How we all laughed, no, chortled at this line. And how we all slowed down the tempo.

From now on efforts to prevent the Germans getting too much coal were stepped up. It was quite the done thing to uncouple a wagon here and there in a train of coal tubs, so that when the locomotive started of the driver found he had left the best part of the train behind. This delayed the train of full tubs reaching the shaft, because the driver had to ensure that everyone of the wagons was coupled. Even so, very often, after checking the train some tubs would become uncoupled by one of us popping out from a dark corner after the driver had passed.

Another ploy of ours was to make it look as if the wagons were full. The reason for this was simple. Each day the Boss Man would tell us how many wagons he wanted from each part of the Section. We were only too willing to oblige the gentleman, only we did not fill them with coal. Rubbish, bits of pit props and other wood, lumps of stone to make up the weight and sprinkle the lot with a thin layer of coal and dust. When Boss Man came round all he could see were apparently full wagons, usually more than he had originally asked for which meant no hour overtime and a pat on the back for being good(?) lads. Funnily enough, none of the overseers seemed to notice what we were doing, nor realise we were pulling the wool over their eyes.

One very big hold up caper we had was when working in the Head Gallery, or in German 'Kopfe Streche'. To reach this we faced a climb of some 700 yards up a 45° slope. This was the 'Farhe Streche' of traffic passage. At the bottom was a jig-pan loader and at intervals up the slope were wooden dams which slowed up the coal going down the fixed chutes.

At the top the coal was loaded into a tip wagon at the coal face, then pushed to the chute and tipped out. However, by hook or by crook we always managed to tip the wagon down as well, about an hour or so into the shift. The time lost in the recovery of the wagon from inside the first dam, came to half a shift or sometimes more.

After pleading innocence, we would complain that the wagon was not very safe and in the end even the Germans came to think the wagon was a danger. The very long and tedious job of recovering it even made the Germans feel a bit uneasy about it. All they could say was go easy with it. They never twigged our game.

Then came the day we matelots decided to go on strike. This caused quite a stir. It took place at a time when all of us were on the morning shift. All, that is, except the one who had a permanent midday shift.

That morning everything went normal until the changing room was reached. After changing into our mining gear we decided to have a 'sit up the top' strike. So, as the different sections were called for, away went the rest but we jolly matelots sat still. Finally there were only the six of us left. Then the Unter Offizier (Corporal) appeared on the scene.

"Wir sint sie?" (Who are you?)

"Wur nicht arbiet heute" (We are not working today)

"Ach! Warum?" (Ah! Why?)

"Kiene essen, kiene arbiet" (No food, no work)

"Donnerwetter! Abteilung? Aus mitt sie. Raus!" (Thunder and lightning. Section? Up you get. Out!)

"Nien, wur sitzen hier. Wur nach haus mitt sie gehen" (No, we are going back to the camp with you)

"Nien nien. Sie gehen arbiet. Raus raus!" (No no. You go to work. Up up!)

So saying he produced his pistol and waved it at us, a rather nasty gleam in his eye. We thought it might be wiser to obey him at this stage, so ever so slowly we got up off the seats and dawdled to the door, out of the dressing room and up to the pithead. Here again we tried to continue the strike to the best of our ability. The cage arrived and the door was opened.

"Rien!" (In)

"Nien. Eine Deutscher kommt. Deutscher vorden Englischer" (No. A German comes. Germans before English)

"Ja. Aberhier ist eine zug. Rien gehen" (Yes. But here is the cage. Get in)

To add force to his words he called over the guards who had accompanied him to the shaft and they unslung their rifles, lifted safety catches and pointed the offending objects at us.

Discretion being the better part of valour, we gave in, though not very gracefully. Our intention on reaching the bottom was to lose ourselves for a goodly time before turning up for work. This plan was doomed to failure, for as if he had read our thoughts, he waved one of the guards to go with us. Needless to say, we still took our time going in and in doing so put the fear of death into the German guard.

One of the direct results of this strike was that for a couple of weeks a pair of guards had to accompany us down the mine and to the coal face, wait there during the shift and bring us back. In addition to this, there was considerable friction between British and Russian P.o.W.'s.

This friction between the two camps of prisoners is explained by the fact that several times during the course of work, our men had lost stuff, maybe a small packet of sandwiches and food was always in full demand, a ruling being that a man who stole food from his fellow prisoners should himself be punished by being deprived of part of his Red Cross issue. The Russians, of course, had no recognised Red Cross, therefore they were not as well off as we were in the way of food.

At one time we would occasionally give one of the Russians a bit of bread, if we had it to spare, but we soon found that this small act brought all the begging Russians in creation on to us, so we packed up doing the Good Samaritan act. Nevertheless, a couple of Russians were caught stealing from our haversacks and that led to a bit of rough stuff and finally downright bad relations. In the end, the Russians had to be kept separate from us and, at the start of the shift, the Russians went down first and they were the last up at the end of the shift. They were not even allowed to work in the same sections as we were eventually.

However, during the 'friendly' period, I had a young Russian working with me. Asking him, through the media of the German language, where he came from and where he was captured, his answer seemed to bear out what the Russian officer had said in Stalag 7A. This young Russian was just 21 years old and was a student at Stalingrad University. As he said, the Germans came along and laid seige to the city. Then all the fit and able males between the ages of 16 to 60 were mustered and Red Army trucks rolled in loaded with uniforms and arms. Without any training whatsoever, they were handed a uniform, rifle and ammunition and were told, "You are now in the Red Army. The Germans are out there, go and stop them."

The war news continued to be good and now we saw something which gave all of us from Italy a good hearty laugh. A large batch of Italian P.o.W.'s appeared on the scene and among them was our old enemy from Camp P.G. 52, 'Farmer Giles', the carabinierre. Now, instead of being the fat, overfed figure he used to be when we had dealings with him, he was thin, his clothes hanging on him in great folds. He had also lost his appetite for bullying others and most of all for confronting those who had promised him a painful death if they ever caught up with him again.

As can well be imagined, there was little love lost between the Italians and ourselves and when passing each other during the course of our work, insults and rude words were the order of the day. More than once one or another of us came to the verge of blows with the Italians, a number of whom still hated the very sight of the British (mostly the Fascist militia), just as we hated the sight of the majority of them.

However, the monotonous routine was relieved now and again by shows put on in the camp, well rehearsed by the inmates who took part in them, on such free Sundays as were available. In fact, I took part in one show which was put on by our hut alone. I played one part as a Cockney pie stall owner in a comedy sketch and also as the great Daily Mirror villain, Captain A.R.P. Reilly-Ffoull. It was that part which got me a role in the Christmas pantomime 'Ali Baber' to which I would add the unofficial rest of the title 'and the forty nasty Nazi's'. Most shows took the form of comic relief, all without exception taking the not too obvious mickey out of the Germans.

Mishaps did occur from time to time in the mine and Section 10a was no better than other sections. At one time I was working in the ffieller, or as we used to call them, the Opera House or Theatre.

In these places the coal was cut from floor to roof, a height of between 6½ and 7½ metres (22 to 25 feet). It was also opened out to a width of about 150 feet. The whole roof was supported by slender wooden pit props. When emptied, they were then filled with sand and water, the water draining off through a dam made of short pit props cemented into the stone floor.

I and another lad were working at the lower end of the ffieller, easing the coal through a narrow opening at the bottom and on to the endless belt. All at once, me being in the upper position of us two, I heard someone shouting and looking up saw the German miner waving his lamp and shouting "RAUS SCHNELL!" (Out quickly!) and then "Dam gebrochen (Dam broken). That was enough for us and we both shot down on to the belt and raced along it like a pair of scalded cats. Off the belt and on to a jig-pan we went, with the water roaring along just a few feet behind and then we passed the opening of the 'fahre streche', breathed a sigh of relief but carried on until we came to a chain hoist and then went upwards.

We were glad to see other faces looking down in anxiety. We were safe at last. However, after repairing the dam it broke after only three days and we repeated our escape routine again. But it was only on going off at the end of the shift that we saw what damage that burst had caused in the main gallery. Wagons were slung about all over the place, pit-props washed away and sand blocking the railway tracks. I went so fast that day, I left my lamp still stuck in a pit prop and my shirt and jacket hanging on a nail close by the end of the belt. When I retrieved them, the water had left them untouched and dry. That was a piece of luck.

During the months we had been working in the mine, I had not so far come unscathed. Apart from the usual run of various bumps, cuts and bruises which most miners receive at times, I had by now been off sick several times through receiving hits on my fingers which had caused me to see our doctor due to the damaged digit swelling and throbbing painfully. Doc's usual treatment was removal of nail from the offended digit.

In the course of time I had, eventually, all but one of my finger and thumb nails removed - one thumb nail twice. Naturally, Doc was on our side and he sought out every possible way to put us sick, even with the German Army Doctor breathing down the back of his neck. I was off with three finger nails for three weeks once. All this was caused by comparatively small knobs of coal unexpectedly falling or rolling down a pile of coal and striking a finger or thumb which was wrapped round the handle of a shovel.

Another time I was on the night shift, when usually not much coal is dug, most jobs were maintenance. This night I was put on the wagon loader which dealt with coal from the 'Overbreak', ie. taken from a higher seam by way of blasting through the solid rock upwards to get at it. A vertical shaft some 80 feet high.

The wagons were moved forward by a compressed air pump which, when there were only empty wagons to move, would shunt them forward so violently that they often jumped off the track. Wisely, I thought, I tried the infernal machine out first and shunted a wagon or two to get the feel of the thing. The coal began to drop, so loading had to begin as well. I had successfully filled three wagons when disaster struck. It was around the bewitching hour of midnight. I had half filled this wagon, an older type than the others and lighter. As I shunted it forward to completely fill it, the wagon moved a bit quicker than I expected, I grabbed at the end of the wagon hoping to stop it, when it left the rails and firmly crunched my right hand between it and the wagon in front.

Managing, I really don't know how, to free my hand, I switched off all the loading machinery, could not make myself heard by those at the seam, so I closed the loading hatch and went in search of the night overseer. He was a smallish gent who reminded me of Grumpy, one of the seven dwarfs. Hence, we used to walk in behind him singing "Heigh Ho, Heigh Ho, it's off to work we go", much to his utter annoyance.

I found him in the ffieller sitting down with his back against a pit prop, fast asleep. Giving him a gentle tap on the shoulder, I stuck my right hand under his nose. All he saw as he opened his eyes was a blood-stained, coal blackened hand. That made him bound to his feet. He took me to the first aid box, produced something he called a bandage and wrapped my fingers in it. Then he found a couple of maintenance men and left me in their tender care to take up to the pithead first aid room.

We finally got to the surface at 05.00 and after showering the dirt off and dressing, the First Aid nurse wrapped my hand in a fresh bandage and I was then packed off in the charge of a sentry to return to the camp. We passed the early shift coming down the road and I waved my hand yelling out "It's a kranker". After our Doctor had seen it he dressed it properly and I had another three weeks rest.

One thing we soon found out about the Germans, they were very one tracked in their minds. When a search was about to be made, most times our interpreter would find out and let us know. If Jerry was looking for weaponry, we would hide them and leave out, in full view, all other things illicit like foodstuffs etc, and vice versa when the search was for all things illicit. The searchers were looking for one thing only and ignored anything else, even though it may be against the rules.

By October 1944, Germany was in a chaotic state. The Russian breakthrough in the east had created havoc on the railways and now most of the trains passing the town were troop trains heading eastward.

Another blow fell on us. We depended a lot on the Red Cross parcels for the wholesome food which, up to now, had kept us going. Without warning the parcels ceased to come through. We had to depend on the German rations.

The one thing which kept our spirits up now were the news bulletins coming through our forbidden radio. The Gestapo had got wind of this radio somehow and tried to locate it. They descended on the camp several times without any warning and at one time were actually standing within feet, if not inches, of the set while one of the operators was using it and still they failed to find it. We must have been very lucky, because the radio functioned right up till the end.

The rapidly disintegrating state of Germany could be clearly seen by the state of their medical supplies, which were practically non-existent, the ever decreasing traffic on the railways and the day and nigh bombardment by air of this part of Germany by British and American planes, almost without interference. They were badly hit by the food situation. The food grew worse and the morale of the miners dropped fast. Out of this grew our stock phrase, "Kiene essen, kiene arbiet" (No food, no work).

Just previous to the start of the collapse of morale among the German miners, I had the most amusing experience with one of the typically arrogant and overbearing type of German.

As is usual with this type, every order they give has to be screamed out at the top of the voice, followed by vile epithets. I was used to this so I took no notice, but as time went on it began to get a bit annoying. I think it was this Germans high pitched voice that annoyed me more than anything else.

This miner lost his temper with all and sundry. We were about 10 metres up a recently started gallery, working on a slope of about 45°. The floor was of shiny stone and gave little or no foothold. Naturally, to drill the shot holes some sort of footing had to be arrange and the German thought to do this by means of a plank placed across the gallery between two of the upright pit props.

No doubt this was a good idea, the question being how to get the plank to the required position first. Mind you, I wasn't much help and after the German had slipped half a dozen times and I had curled up laughing at him, he really lost his temper. Finally he fixed his plank, climbed up on to it, grabbed his pick and took a mighty swipe at the coal face, missed and all but came off the plank. More mirth from me.

That did it. Raving mad, he ordered me away from him and to go and get an electric drill. Still chortling, I went. I found a drill, As I touched it I felt a slight shock.

"Oh-oh" thought I and knowing my electrics, said "This monster had an earth on it and if he grabs it and switches on, he'll get one almighty wallop. That ought to teach him a few manners."

So, with great care, I picked up the offending machine by way of it's rubber covered cable and carted it back to my offensive German miner. By the time I got back, he had worked himself into quite a sweat and had knocked a few starting holes in the coal face.

With his usual diplomacy he roared at me to hand him the machine, reaching from the plank at the same time. Carefully, so as not to touch any metal part, I handed up the drill. He grabbed it by the metal handle without any effect as yet. The wooden plank was for the time being preventing him from getting a shock he would feel.

Now came the testing time. Would he get a belt? He inserted the bit. Now he raised the drill and poised it in front of one of his start holes, leaned forward, inserted the drill and switched on.

I don't think I shall ever forget what happened next, it was so comical, just what one would see in a slap-stick comedy film. The drill started and dug into the coal face and there appeared to jam. My German miner let out a howl of pure anguish, leapt into the air, still pressing the switch of the machine and the drill started to revolve round the bit, carrying a frenzied German with it before the combined weights of man and drill tore the bit loose from the coal face.

Naturally I was in the doghouse for laughing and just as naturally, and rightfully, I got the blame for bringing a faulty machine.

The outcome though, was that for the rest of the shift, I had a very subdued German in charge of me. He dared not complain or try to get me punished in any way, I could always plead that the machine was in order when I got it or that it was the only one available.

Now that the Red Cross parcels were held up, our efforts to reduce coal production increased. The British Medical Officer in the camp did what he could by putting men sick on odd days, but he was tied to a great extent by the presence near by of a large German Military Hospital. If there were too many sick, up would come the German M.O. and immediately some 60% to 70% were put fit again, sometimes more. If a man was off sick for too long according to German standards, he had to attend the German Military Hospital, with the nett result that in most cases he was pronounced fit and sent back to work.

There were a couple of cases of guard trouble during 1944. The first case concerned a small shrill voiced guard whom we called the 'Squeaker'. His persistent squeaking and cries of "schnell, schnell, los, los" (faster, move) got on our nerves. He was a typical fault finder. Even the short walk down to the mine from the camp he made a trial. One could not stop even to pull up a sock without him making a song and dance out of it.

The answer was a strong complaint. We complained. No reply. We made another stronger complaint, with this time the Doctor sticking his oar in and stirring it up. This time there was a reply and before we knew it the "Squeaker" had a draft to the Eastern Front and had left our merry throng.

The second case could be called that of the irate Unteroffizier. The occurrence happened one morning as were mustering for the morning shift. This Unteroffizier strode round and into the huts rounding up the morning shift, hustling them outside. In one of the huts one of our lads was still drinking a cup of tea. There was still plenty of time in actual fact before we were due to leave, but this German wanted to get us out of his way.

Into the hut strode the Unteroffizier. "Raus, raus, schnell raus schnell". Our man looked at him disdainfully. Then he carried on drinking. This made the German more irate. He let fly a long string of oaths before making a further order to clear the hut. Still our lad carried on drinking. His tea was almost gone by now anyway. The last mouthful drunk, he casually ambled to his bed to collect his haversack. The German was by now livid with rage. As our lad turned to walk through the door, the German drew his bayonet and made a vicious stab at the lad's back. Our man saw the move out of the corner of his eye and took avoiding action, at the same time instinctively throwing out a hand to ward off the blow. The bayonet went into his hand, the point narrowly missing causing further damage to the lad's back, his clothing being pierced by the bayonet point.

There was nothing for it, but to put the lad off sick. The incident caused a call for reprisals against the German, but somehow the authorities did nothing about it, saying the guard was acting within his rights with a recalcitrant prisoner. That was not good enough for us. We wanted revenge and quick. We got it very soon.

Somehow we had to get rid of this Unteroffizier. But how? One sure thing we knew the Germans did not like a thief. Suppose he could be branded a thief, then he would be sent away, probably to the Russian front. The answer to this problem now became simple. The Red Cross parcel issue was the ideal time, but it had to be when this particular German attended the opening of the parcels. One of the camp staff was a good sleight of hand merchant and another of the camp staff was to be the one who would inspect his parcel when he got it and complain that it was short of a certain item.

The plot went off perfectly. The camp staff member drew his parcel, then apparently remembered something and sorted over his parcel. The usual block of chocolate was missing. He demanded to know what had happened to his chocolate, where was it.

The Feldwebel officiating at the parcel issue then took over. He ordered a search of the discarded wrappings. Nothing was found. Next, under great protest from the staff involved, he ordered a search of the British personnel engaged in unwrapping the parcels. Still nothing was found. then our own Camp R.S.M. protested that the British had been searched, so it was only fair that the German guards and personnel who had been present at the unpacking and issuing of the parcels should be searched. He argued that fair was fair and it was only right that as our boys had been subjected to a search, so should the Germans, if only to clear the air.

The Feldwebel, being a very fair minded man and not wishing to have a heap of trouble on his hands, finally agreed to the idea. He offered himself as the first victim for the search. Of course he was clean and knew it. The guards came in one at a time, with no sign of the missing chocolate and then, almost the last, came the Unteroffizier. One can quite well imagine his honest surprise when the Feldwebel put his hand in the Corporal's jacket pocket and withdrew the missing block of chocolate.

There lay only one course open to the Germans. Get rid of the offending Corporal. Despite his protestations of innocence he was sent, as was usual for a punishment, to the Russian Front. That was the last we heard or saw of him.

Late in December we started to get a few parcels through. Christmas was almost upon us and the International Red Cross at Geneva made sure we got our Christmas food parcels through on time, even if it meant making the delivery themselves.

A pantomime had been arranged for Christmas Day, two performances, one in the afternoon and one in the evening. I, with pride, took quite a large part in this pantomime, 'Ali Baber' though how they worked out that I should be the extremely wicked Uncle Ebenazi I don't know. Still, the Germans never fell in they were taking the mickey out of them as usual.

One other funny incident took place a short time before Christmas. This concerned the Still that was in operation. We were allowed German beer which was as strong and intoxicating as gnats water, so we had to provide some other means of getting a little merry. A little Schnapps was obtained from various miners by a little bit of crafty bargaining, or bartering, French cigarettes being the usual medium, but to get a good sizzling brew, that we had to produce ourselves.

The brew was made by collecting the dried fruit received in the Canadian Red Cross parcels and in some British parcels, soaking it and fermenting it with a few of our precious raw potatoes and putting the result through the Still. The process took quite a long time and if we were caught at it there was hell to pay from the Germans.

It became known that the Germans knew there was a Still in the camp. The Germans made a sudden raid. The Still was captured and borne off in triumph by the Feldwebel and his cohorts. Not for long though. Off went our Camp Interpreter, one Bombardier Jim Wadey. Within ten minutes he was bearing the Still back into the camp and handing it over to its keeper.

Looking back over the time spent in that camp, many and varied were the local contraptions used for various jobs. One of these contraptions was the patent water heater run from the electric mains. This was a simple affair, consisting of two tins, one smaller than the other and insulated from each other by a piece of dry wood. This would be plugged into the mains, the elements lowered carefully into the dixie of water, care being taken not to let the elements touch the sides of the dixie or mug if either were metal, and then results awaited.

Boiling water used to be obtained in about three to four minutes as opposed to six to ten minutes using the coal fire stove top. There was a snag with this water heater. Every time it was used, all the lights in the camp would dim down to half power because of the excessive load put on the mains and the German electricians were at a complete loss as to the cause of this phenomena. They never did find the answer to that problem.

In the summer months we had been annoyed by a local German girl who was friendly with one of the guards. She used to come into the mine when we were mustering ready to be marched back to the camp after the morning shift and parade her doubtful charms to us by mincing up and down in front of us, looking at us as if we were something nasty that had crawled out from under a piece of mouldy German cheese. She soon put an end to her capers when one of the lads remarked in fluent German to his chums, "She was parading up and down like the Queen of the mine, only she reminded him more of a Piccadilly whore".

That reminds me of the fellow who was working in the separation department. Apparently he was taken by the charms (or otherwise) of a certain wench also working in the same area. His trouble, being a bit thick, was that he could not speak German. Not a word. He longed to be able to make some sort of contact with the aforesaid wench, so he asked one of the other lads how he could break the ice. He was told, just walk over to her and say "Bist du ein jungfrau?" and he would get an answer.

Making sure he could spit out the short speech, over to the wench he trots. Catching her attention he then proceeded with the phrase he had been told to say. The result was startling, for him. She swiped him one across the face.

Stumbling back to his mates, red-faced in more ways than one, the imprint of one female hand still showing and tingling, he asked what went wrong. Then his mates asked him what he had said. What you told me was the lad's answer as his accomplices in crime burst out laughing. Then they reproachfully said, "Did you really say that?". "Yes" came the reply. Once more a burst of laughter, and then they said sorrowfully like, "Fancy asking a girl like her if she's a virgin". It did pay to learn a bit of basic German.

If my memory serves me right, it was in October that one of the lads decided to escape. Although the area had been declared a 'Death Zone', ie. any stranger or suspicious person could be shot on sight. The escape took place from the mine, the escapee using a wagon for his transport to the top, whereupon, taking a considerable risk, he hopped out and walked off without a challenge, so it seems. Apparently he was never caught.

In the camp we covered his escape by 'running the rabbit' at all musters. This ploy meant that a short fellow would get in the middle rank of the five files and having been counted, would then smartly nip along behind the others into a convenient blank space and be counted again. This caper went on for about ten days before some disgruntled guard decided to look along the lines instead of walking round and along the front or back as usual. Of course the rabbit could not run and we were one person short. Oh dear!

The Russians had not been too quiet either. Although we were in technically two separate camps, we were only divided from them by a high fence heavily festooned with barbed wire. One thing we did know was that the Polish Underground Resistance were somewhere in the vicinity, they had tried to contact us in the hopes that we might be persuaded into making a mass breakout. We, quite naturally said no thanks, having weighed up all the possibilities and deciding that if we did, the Posterns (German Home Guard on Camp Duties) would have a field day collecting our scalps after they had shot us all.

It would appear that the Russians were not so careful about such matters and did not think things through like we did. What actually happened was like something out of an American war movie, only in this case the (American) heroes were the German Posterns. Without any warning or intimation that anything was about to happen, a mass of Russians made a mad rush for the fences around their part of the camp. There came a shout and then the rattle of light machine gun fire plus the crack of rifles. The Posterns, in their elevated positions in the watch towers, had seen the move and, being armed with the machine guns, had a merry time being heroes and shooting unarmed men. Some bodies were left on the wire for some days before being removed. We also heard that some more Russians were taken into their washroom and shot out of hand.

Christmas passed and January 1945 arrived. It had been very noticeable that the traffic on the railway had dropped to a bare few trains each day, but at night there were a few more trains, only these were travelling eastwards. One or two troop trains passed ruing the day, but most preferred night travel.

The news over our secret radio had become very encouraging. The Russians were sweeping in from the east and were racing toward Berlin, our troops were on German soil and the fight was being carried on well in the Fatherland.

We had heard of the bomb plot against Hitler and how he was supposed to have survived. Somehow we were a bit doubtful. The reason for this was that from the time that Hitler was supposed to have recovered from the effects of the bomb, all his speeches were given late at night or in the early hours of the morning. How could very many people listen to a speech given at 12.30am, if they had to rise for work at 4am or 5am. Sleep would just about be impossible, especially as our bombers were creating havoc in night raids. Not only that, the speeches were rather garbled, containing bits and pieces of past speeches. It appeared to us that somebody was trying to keep alive the Hitler legend, and these supposed speeches of his were in fact bits and pieces of previous speeches of Hitler which had been recorded and the bits were being edited so as to produce another speech, or in fact, several speeches. We believed Hitler had been killed by that bomb and even now, after much evidence had been produced to prove that he died in the Berlin bunker, I still have my personal doubts about it.

By the middle of January, traffic on the railway had virtually ceased and in the mine there were a noticeable number of Germans going absent. The Russian troops were not so very far from us now and we were wondering how long it would be before they reached us and whether the Germans would just abandon us to our fate or move us to a place of comparative safety before handing us over.

We were soon to know the answer to that one. About 19th or 20th January work virtually ceased in the mine. Going to work was a farce. Few German miners turned up for work and it became the case of one German to four or five British. The Germans seemed not to care whether any work was done or not and only a token amount of coal was sent to the top.

This was the time when the mine and the camp came under bombardment from the Russian Army for the first time. All the camp lights were doused which meant no lights in any of the rooms, but we got over that one by bringing our carbide lamps up from the mine and using them as room illumination. Of course the carbide was in short supply and had to be carefully hoarded.

During the days between 20th and 25th January, several air raids were made in the vicinity by Russian aircraft and by 24th January, only a token handful of miners turned up for work. None of these were party members and they were those who refused to flee before the Russian advance.

25th January was the fateful day. I had the morning shift, went below and did no work whatsoever. I just waited for the shift to finish. The midday shift went down, but were recalled to the top within the hour. The word had come to shift the camp lock, stock and barrel.

CHAPTER TEN

The Great March

25th January 1945. The morning shift had arrived back in camp and they and the night shift had been told to get packed and be ready to leave by 18.30. The afternoon shift had yet to arrive back in the camp and as far as we knew, were still waiting to come up, even though word had been sent for them to get back to the camp.

All was hustle and bustle. The remaining stock of Red Cross parcels had been issued, two parcels per man, one a British and one a Canadian parcel. These parcels plus any food we had been able to put by and anything left over from our daily rations from the Germans, was the only food we would be able to take with us and had to be jealously guarded.

I had converted a kitbag, sent by my parents whilst in Italy, into a haversack by sewing on a spare pair of braces to be used as adjustable shoulder straps and by removing the tie strings from the top of the bag, had made a tie rope which went round the bag once the open end had been rolled down to form the top cover.

In this bag I had packed everything else that I had apart from that which I was wearing and I had put as much on as I could wear and still walk with some ease. Outside the snow lay in deep drifts. Marching in that would be very hard going with a loaded bag on your back, so some other form of transport had to be found.

That answer was simple. Sleds! Ingenuity and commonsense came to the fore. From literally nothing, sleds of all shapes and sizes started to appear. Old boxes, odd lengths of wood and boards from our bunks all went into the making of these assorted, but practical machines, each capable of carrying all the extras of two person at least. At the outset they carried all our gear, with the food stowed out of sight under our personal gear and saved us a whole lot of puff and pant.

Due partly to the lateness with which the afternoon shift had arrived back in the camp and partly due to an altercation between the Germans and our British M.O. over one of our fellows lying in the sick quarters with double pneumonia, we did not muster until 19.00 hours.

This argument was over whether the lad should be moved. Our doctor said he had to remain where he was, if he was moved he would die and that there were volunteers from among his medical staff to stay with the lad. The Germans said NO! The man must leave the camp with the rest of us. They got their way, as can well be guessed. So he was placed on the Ambulance wagon, horse drawn, quite naturally and covered with as much warm gear as could be found.

British P.o.W.'s from other camps in the area had by now filtered into the camp and there were now 1,200 of us. We finally started out in a long straggling line leading the column into the freezing night.

Down the hill from the camp we marched, passing the mine where we had been not very hard at work that morning and on into the town of Klausberg, the centre of the local mining activities. None of us were sorry to see the last of that place, or to see the mine disappear into the darkness behind us.

The intense cold was reaching out for us now, we could feel it as it found all those tiny gaps and odd loose folds in our clothing. Only the fact that we were keeping a brisk pace would keep us warm now. The fast pace soon had us puffing and panting under the strain of hauling a loaded sled in the deep snow. Even with two pulling the pace began to tell and one could not afford to get stuck in a snowdrift.

The rumbling of the Russian artillery was loud in our ears now, the Russians being, in fact, only a bare 10 miles away and already occupying some of the mining towns just over the border in Poland. Our objective, we were told, was to get through a 50 mile wide gap between two prongs of a Russian pincer movement, one prong coming up through Czechoslovakia and the other a thrust from the Russian forces in the north who were now a bare 40 miles from Berlin. The crossing of the River Oder had to take place at the town of Rattibor.

The Germans had an almost insuperable job on their hands. Their task was to clear some 28,000 P.o.W.'s from the area. There was confusion, compounded by the presence of retreating German forces from the eastern front. 28,000 was only an estimated figure for the number of P.o.W.'s milling around.

We carried on marching until midnight, with a ten minute stop every two hours. At the first halt I, and I presume many others, discovered that it was not a wise thing to do to sit down, at least not for longer than 30 seconds. Movement just had to be kept going, if not you froze up. Thus, having tried out a sit down at the first halt and finding it most difficult to get up again and moving, because the intense cold soon affected idle limbs, the blood started to freeze. To move was agony until eventually the affected limbs thawed out through movement. Thus, on all following halts, I studiously kept my arms and legs moving.

When we finally came to a halt about midnight, we found we had met up with another column of prisoners. Then came a lot of shuffling about and sorting out of different nationalities and, eventually, we were under way again, us British leading as usual when a fast pace was required. The column now consisted of 1,200 British, 3,000 Greeks and Balkanites, and 5,000 Russians. Soon the column became stretched out over a very long distance.

During the night we passed through many small villages and a few small towns. At dawn we were halted outside a small church in a tiny village. During the night, our lad on the 'Krank Wagon' as our ambulance became known to us, had died. The local parson had been contacted and when he arrived the body of our lad was carried, covered by a shroud, into the church, where the priest made a solemn promise that the boy would be given a Christian burial with full rites. He would look after the body and get a proper coffin.

After this stop we carried on marching again, the usual routine of two hours marching and ten minutes rest. Towards evening the snow began to fall again and visibility fell to little more than 100 yards. Now we were on the outskirts of Glywitz. With the sound of the Russian guns still loud in our ears, now slightly muffled by the falling snow, we marched through the town. Night was upon us by the time we left the town and it was here, outside Glywitz, that we became mixed up with a part of a dispirited, despairing army.

The scene can only be described as chaotic. There were fresh troops going forward toward the front line and wearied, dishevelled, gaunt faced troops coming from the front line. There was defeat, exhaustion, disillusion in their looks. They were the lucky ones, still alive and in one piece. They hardly cast a glance at either us or the long line of horse drawn wagons which looked like farm wagons, that both they and we were passing.

These wagons were full of casualties. This was the ambulance section. The sight was simply shocking. How anybody could survive in those carts I do not know. The scene still lives in my memory.

The wounded were heaped into the carts and had no blankets that seemed any good, merely tattered old blankets, pieces of sacking, tattered greatcoats and any other covering that would serve. Of medical supplies there seemed nil and bandages seemed to be torn up strips of sheets or the like.

We could see some of the wounded writhing in agony and there was no way their torment could be eased. Some were obviously on their way out of this world, and in at least three of the wagons there were living among the dead. It made me wonder just how many of those wounded would ever survive, if any would finally get into a hospital alive. Judging by what I saw that evening, not many.

We did notice that most of those troops moving into the front line were wearing snow capes and their faces were almost as white as the capes themselves. Some motorised light and heavy armour was in evidence, but seemed to be paralysed by a common lack of fuel.

Leaving all the confusion behind us, we moved on to a secondary road. We had not gone far down this road when there came the sound of a plane diving. It seemed to be diving directly at the column so, doing what comes naturally under those circumstances, we all took off and dived head first into the ditches at either side of the road. A loud bang came from somewhere ahead. Pulling myself out of the ditch, or rather the snow in it, I took a look round and then burst out into rather unseemly mirth, for all round me there were pairs of legs sticking up out of the snow, above which legs, slowly appeared the rest of the bodies the legs belonged to. It was like something out of the 'Three Stooges'. Then I realised that I must have presented the same sort of sight. Word came back from the front of the column that something had exploded a short distance in front of them, but there were no casualties or damage.

From now on the marching continued practically unbroken, two hours march, ten minutes break. The sounds of battle faded in the distance behind us. We ate when we could, not that there was much to eat. As for drink, that was almost an impossibility. All we could do under these circumstances was to try to melt a cup of fresh clean snow in a cup, but invariably before the snow melted the break ended, so no drink. The answer was to try to knock an icicle off a roof end when we passed through a village and suck it.

All along the route, at every conceivable moment, there were members of our column slipping off out of the marching mass in an attempt to escape, in the vain hope that they might be rescued by the

Russians. In most cases the straggling column and poor visibility assisted these escapees, but what they had not thought of was the Germans being smart and just by chance thinking about that problem. Obviously they had, because they had a 'Sweeper Upper' detachment at the rear of the column for just that purpose, sweep up all the would be escapers. Those were returned to the column when we reached the Oder crossing at Rattibor.

Weariness began to overtake us now, although we still kept up the momentum of the pace. Then came a very welcome break of about four hours. We had come through a village and were halted in a field on the outskirts. Fires were lit with what brushwood could be found, in order that we may make a hot brew.

Now there came a problem. How best to protect our food supplies from the Russians who had left their column and were now mingling with our lads, ever on the lookout for an unguarded food store. These Russians knew we had food and that was why they were trying to make themselves as inconspicuous as possibly by mingling with us. They were partly successful in their tactics, for one or two of our lads did in fact lose their food supplies. The trouble was to catch the light-fingered grub thieves and make an example of them, they were experts at the job.

So far, the pace had been quite fast, enough to play out the strength of some of the weaker members, two or three were already on the ambulance wagon with the Doctor attending them. Now, at this long halt there came a further casualty. This lad had sat in a shelter he had rigged over his sled and had fallen asleep, a most dangerous thing to do in these circumstances. When awakened by his chums, he found himself frozen into the position he had dozed off in. His comrades carried him in this frozen position over to the ambulance wagon for treatment and finally thawed out none the worse for his experience, but wiser.

The forced march continued for another full day and night. Finally we arrived at Rattibor and as we passed the railway marshalling yard there, had thoughts of our journey being continued aboard a train, even if it meant freight wagons once more. On second thoughts, after seeing what had happened to the rolling stock and locomotives, we decided that walking was best. There were no moveable stock, all had been ruined, probably by an air raid by the R.A.F. as they were the most accurate bomb droppers.

Passing the railway yard we then came to our crossing point of the Oder. Not a very big or wide bridge, the Oder at this point was quite narrow. Here we stopped for about two hours. During this wait, all the would-be escapers were returned to the column. A Russian who thought that this would be an opportune time to get away was spotted by an alert guard and a couple of shots rang out in the still morning air and the Russian went down and lay unmoving in the snow. I had watched the whole incident from beginning to end.

We moved on over the bridge. Most of us by this time were almost at the end of our tether. We wanted sleep more than anything else, although hot food and drink would have been a boon.

The continuous white glare from the snow caused a great deal of trouble for us. Constantly having to look at it began to have a mesmeric effect. A great tiredness came over a person and the only thing they wanted to do was sleep and if they succumbed to it, they would fall asleep although still walking. I had cause to remember this. Soon after leaving the River Oder behind, my travelling partner, Rifleman Joe Osborne, veered toward me and started to lean on me, so I just shoved him away, thinking he had accidently blundered into me. The next I knew, I had the whole weight of our sled and he was leaning on me again only more heavily this time. Glancing around at him, I saw his eyes were closed, so I gave him a shake. He came to after a fashion and started to take a bit of the strain of the sled, but after a few minutes he was leaning on me again, more heavily now and I had the full weight of the sled.

Now the full import of what was wrong hit me. There was only one thing to do, so I took the necessary action. I gave him a full-blooded thump on the chin with my fist. That really woke him up and I dodged back a bit anticipating a retaliatory bunch of fives. Lucky for me head been so far gone that he just looked at me as if he had just awakened and quietly thanked me for waking him. I gave him my apologies later for having thumped him one.

We continued marching throughout the rest of the day and it was late evening, well after dark, that we came to a farm. The Germans stopped us here, then they herded us into barns. Once sentries had been placed, we were allowed to wander out into the farmyard and that was when I and some others indulged in a rare luxury, a wash in snow.

It was sheer heaven to remove some of our top gear and then rub snow into our faces and over hands and wrists. The unwashed feeling of the last few days just seemed to drop away. Although this washing in snow was very refreshing, it was impossible to remove all the dirt and grime that had accumulated and we all had to be content with removing what we could.

The surprise of the evening now came. The Germans had managed to arrange a hot meal here, the usual hot boiled potatoes and with the added luxury of some hot ersatz coffee. Our spirits were now bolstered up with hot food and drink inside us.

Once the meal was finished, we settled down for the night. The straw we were to use as bedding felt like a feather bed under the present circumstances. Having chosen which part of the stack of straw we wished to make our bed in, then came the problem of removing some articles of clothing. Boots came high on the list.

Trying to get my boots off proved to be a hard job. First, my feet were so cold I could not feel them and secondly, my boots were frozen solid. What had caused this was that initially the warmth from my feet had also warmed the boots, thus when walking in powdery snow, that warmth had melted the snow and the water thus made had gradually soaked into the leather of my boots, seeped through into the outer part of the four pairs of socks I was wearing and as that slowly cooled my feet so the boots in their wet state froze. Hence very cold feet.

We had found that the best way to sleep and keep warm was to get together in groups of three or four, the more the merrier so to speak. Then half the blankets could be used as under sheets and the remainder as top sheets and with all tightly bunched together more heat became generated and the warmer we were. So stuffing my boots with straw, I then placed them under the straw I was using as a pillow, hoping they would thaw out during the night.

The following morning started two weeks of hard marching, from early morning to late at night. It also became two weeks of terror and ruthless slaughter by the guards of the Russians. Nobody knew until now that some SS guards had joined the column and were bringing up the rear. They were there to ensure that nobody got away.

Although on most days we, the British column, would lead, on some days the Russians would take pole position. That was when we could see what happened when a Russian fell out of line. The Russians were definitely feeling the pace and they were the ones who fell out of the column and paid for it with their lives.

Every day during this period, we heard shots being fired, sometimes singly and sometimes in a fusillade. I can recall seeing some of the Russians being shot, they only had to move a few yards from the column and without warning came the shots and more dead bodies were left lying in ditches, alongside the road or in fields. I lost count, probably because there were bodies of those shot by the guards of a column ahead of us. I can remember seeing one dead Russian by the roadside frozen in the kneeling position with his hands held together in front of his chest as if in prayer. He had been shot through the temple.

The Russians began to get crafty. Instead of taking the risk of falling out of the column in open country, they resorted to hanging on until they were in a village or small town and then collapse in the middle of it knowing the SS were not so daft as to shoot them in front of civilians. I do not think this ploy did the Russians much good, because the SS merely arranged for them to be wheeled away, ostensibly to join the column, but in actuality to be executed at a lonely spot along the road.

On an average we were marching about 55kms per day. The distance varied from day to day, sometimes less sometimes more. This is an average of 34½ miles per day. The terrain we were travelling over became varied. As we approached the forested areas of the border country between Silesia and Czechoslovakia the snow became softer and stickier. It became an effort to drag the sled, it stuck and slithered sideways, or buried its nose in a small particularly soft drift. The roads were not much better. In some cases we were using roads that were little better than cart tracks. But at the end of each day we could look forward to some kind of shelter for the night and at least a handful of hot potatoes to help fill our empty stomachs.

At the end of this fortnight we arrived at a farm not far from the Czech border and here we stopped for five days. The excuse given was that the Germans were awaiting permission to march us across the border and through Czechoslovakia. It did give the Doctor a chance to attend to some of the minor ills that had beset some of us and gave us a chance to get our breath and strength back again.

The time came for us to continue to march. We now, at last, crossed the border into Czechoslovakia and it was just like passing into a totally different kind of world. The road led downhill to a village and as we slowly moved lower, so the snow grew thinner until it disappeared as if by magic.

This meant that sleds were no longer the order of the day and had to be disposed of. My modified kitbag now came into its own. It was still very heavy, being filled with kit I thought would be needed. However it made marching that much easier.

About now I began to feel that something was not quite right with my left foot. Each time the column stopped I found it getting harder and harder to get going again properly. Even a few minutes made no difference, I required time to find the right step to ease the pain.

I continued on as the daily marches were of much less duration now. The Czech population in village after village as we passed through showed us kindness and practical sympathy for our plight by pressing gifts of bread and cakes on us, for which we were most grateful, because our food situation had become critical.

Somewhere around this time, our straggling mixed column met up with another similar column and at this point the two columns were sorted out into four different groups, British, Commonwealth, Russian, Greek and Slavs. The column now became 1,000 British and about the same Aussies and Kiwis, while the Russians were all bunched together and the same with the Greek and Slavs. Then we parted company and went each on its own route.

The first large town we came to was Pardubice and here again the reception by the local people was fantastic. We passed through here and the route began to unfold itself. The next large town was Konnigratz, then Jungbuntzlau, when we found the route led toward Prague. As before the reception from the locals was terrific, always managing somehow to press food into our hands, although we knew that they themselves must have been very short of it.

Somewhere along this route we were met by Swiss representatives of the International Red Cross, who told us there were Red Cross parcels waiting to be issued to us at our next stopping place. We now knew that an eye was being kept on our movements, which gave us a bit of comfort. This was good news and so were the cigarettes issued with the parcels. We had all, I think, been out of smokes for a while now and without a smoke, our empty tums made themselves felt.

The German Medical High Command must have decided to do the right thing and send a doctor to do what he could with any casualties we had and check up on the general health situation among us. We had reached one village and as the pain in my foot had now become almost unbearable, the lads around me forced me to go and see the doctor. My left foot had an angry red blotch and I was immediately put on the 'Krank Wagon'. I had a poisoned foot, caused by mild frostbite.

March came and with it blustery cold winds. Now I was to go down with another ailment, either dysentery or enteritis, I know not which. For the next ten days I can remember very little, only the care of others dragging me off and on the Krank Wagon. Most of the time I was out to the world, supported by others in the wagon I gathered later. I do vaguely remember once having a burnt spud thrust into my mouth and being told to scoff it quick. Then once on the wagon, coming round and spotting some hares scampering along the road side and muttering something about 'Mad March Hares'.

Our 1,000 had been split into companies of 250 each and each company into five platoons of 50 men each. This made for much better organisation with regards to evening quarters, usually one company of 250 into one barn. We were still making for Prague and before we actually saw any sight of it, I came out of my sickness and started to take an active interest in things once more.

Passing round Prague, which appeared to take all of seven days, because all that time all signposts had pointed in the direction of Prague. Again here we saw the results of some of the Allied bombing raids. A railway marshalling yard we passed close to Prague had a display of locomotives which would never haul another train. They had boiler tubes sprouting from out their smoke boxes, caved in boilers and were in a generally unfit condition. We continued marching, via Pilsen and Marienbad in Sudatenland, coming to rest at Weiden in Bavaria, and there we stopped for the next two weeks.

This was a most welcome break, probably the best one we had been given up to date. The Doctor now had ample time to attend to all his patients and to treat them to the best of his ability, given the circumstances. Doc lanced my foot and it was miraculously cured before we were ready to move off again and I was able to hoof it once more. (I needed the exercise too after being stuck on that wagon).

Once again food became a problem. The farmer, a miserable old so and so, was very loathe to give his precious stock of spuds to a shower of Englanders. However, the might of the Military bore down upon him and he, very reluctantly, allowed his spud clamp to be opened for our use. We were warned not to attempt to pilfer any of farmer's other stock, not that much notice was taken of that order.

Another potato store was found by kind permission of one of the farm girls who, it appeared, was quite willing to open the store providing she was not implicated in the following proceedings should we be fount out. None of us wanted that to happen. We raided it to obtain extra spuds for a special boil-up later in the day, a sort of evening meal. Old Misery never suspected anything until one day he decided to make an inspection of his spare hoard of potatoes. What he found made him blow his top.

All hell was now let loose. He accused us of stealing and worse. He went really crackers when he saw one of our lads with some recently procured potatoes. Livid with Teutonic rage he called in the local Gestapo, an unwise move if anything. We now fell back on our old sleight of hand trick. On being questioned, our young British Gentleman replied that he had traded a bar of English toilet soap for the spuds. This bemused the not so very bright Gestapo men. Not knowing quite what to do or who to believe, they decided to search the premises just to find out the right answer. There, lo and behold, in one of the farms outer wash places, there lying in full view was this bar of English toilet soap, very little used.

Farmer protested his innocence strongly, claiming that he had been framed, that he knew nothing of the soap and how he would never trade with an Englander Gefangener. Our looks of hurt innocence at his outburst must have fooled the Gestapo, but for our farmer worse was to come. Whilst searching the farm, the Gestapo had come across other hidden and undeclared goods and farm produce, all of which should have gone into the communal store. Hoarding of food stuff etc, was forbidden most strongly and no amount of snivelling and Heil Hitlering helped in the least, off he went to the local Gestapo lock-up. We never saw him again and his fate remains unknown.

At this point, I wish to go back to the cold windy days of March. Soon after the new formations of prisoners had been made, we came upon a column of German troops. We stopped a short distance from them and had plenty of time to study them closely. This company of the Wehrmacht were youngsters, most looked as if they were fresh out of school and some looked no more than 14 or 15 years old. A more frightened lot would be hard to find. Fear shone in their faces. God knows how much training they had done for the job they were supposedly about to do. I thought, had the Germans got to such a bad stage that school kids had to be sent out to fight? My heart went out to those poor kids.

Then on the other side of us, coming down a pathway, were a group of about 50 or perhaps a few more, concentration camp prisoners, Jewish I imagine. They were nothing more than walking skeletons, with no covering other than the prisoner uniform they were wearing. Another sight of Hitler's inhumanity to man.

It was now April and the weather had changed to bright sun and cloudless skies. Once again we set off into the unknown, now in our companies and platoons. This system became a firm favourite because we had the same guards all the time and got to know them quite well. Our platoon was lucky, for we had very pleasant and cheerful guards, quite willing to give us any information we wished. They knew the war was on its last legs and seemed quite happy about it.

Now there was order where once it had been chaos. We were refreshed and soon got into the swing of marching and there we were marching as if we were the guards and not the prisoners.

Soon we were passing through the outskirts of Weiden and then we turned south onto an autobahn. At last a decent road to march along, so the pace dropped into a steady rhythm which took us along at a fair pace. We had gone two or so miles along the road when ahead of us we spotted a large formation of aircraft. They were fighter planes and obviously on the lookout for columns of Germans, on foot or motorised. The flash of a white star on the wings told us they were American.

The order was quickly passed not to break ranks or dive for cover unless they did actually make an offensive run at us. The German guards had closed in among us so as not to be conspicuous. One can always argue over the folly or otherwise of such orders and it was a severe test of our nerves. We knew we had been seen, for two planes suddenly peeled off from the formation.

They came spiralling down towards us, but we still kept our steady pace and formation. Then one plane started to come lower with the second plane circling above watching like a hawk. Our nerves were on edge and it was with the utmost difficulty that we kept on going without faltering. Down still further came the first plane, until he was barely a hundred feet above us, then veering to one side he made a run past us. We breathed sighs of relief and as he passed down our left side, he waved at us.

The pilot turned, came back over us climbing a little as he did so, then turning again he came right down, flying along our left side again at about 50 feet. As he passed we were waving again and we could see right into the cockpit as he banked slightly and gave us the thumbs up sign, then a waggle of his wings and away to join the other plane still hanging about above us. We noticed afterwards that the two planes were circling above us for a long time, then finally left.

The formation were probably acting on some previous instructions and had most likely been told to investigate moving columns before attacking, as it had become known to the Allies that large scale movements of P.o.W.'s were taking place and again may have been checking on our direction of travel and probable daily destination.

The rest of the formation had flown on toward Weiden. Suddenly, from somewhere way behind us there came an almighty bang. On looking back we could see huge clouds of smoke rising from what appeared to be an oil storage dump. That huge explosion must have rocked Weiden to its very foundations.

The marches each day now became much easier, some days only 10kms, other days perhaps 15kms. So we marched onward and when we were billeted for the night, went out and raided any hen houses there were available, or any other store that might contain food. We lite fires before it became dark for two very good reasons. First was to get a hot brew going, secondly to let our aerial watchdogs know exactly where we were. The same procedure in the morning, a smoky fire for the dawn patrol to see.

We first made toward Nuremberg, but had to turn back, then we made for Regensburg, but the Americans got there first, so it was back to the drawing board again. The route now took us along the road to Vienna, but I do not think our minds were on Strauss waltzes. All along the way there were plenty of evidence of the strength of the Allies fighting power. The Germans were certainly catching a packet. At one place, there was a mile long trail of wreckage of what had once been a motorised column. Caught in the open, with no cover except the trees at the side of the road, the column had been completely wiped out. Burned out and wrecked vehicles lay in the ditches either side of the road, or rammed against trees into which they had collided, light A.A. guns with twisted barrels pointed at the sky.

All around us, although it was spring and the plant life was beginning to show, there were trees with the bark stripped off where they had been hit by aircraft cannon fire and shot up cars burned out and the skeletons of lorries lying in a higgledy-piggledy fashion among the bomb craters.

One evening, we had just arrived at our stop for the night and had just started to light our fires, when the sunset patrol came over. Suddenly they dived down on the road off which we had so recently come. There came the rattle of heavy cannon fire, a loud bang and then the planes were up and away. Somebody who was near the road ran out to see what had happened and came haring back calling for assistance. The small column of Germans had been using horse drawn carts and one of the horses had been killed.

In next to no time that poor old horse had been hauled into our quarters, skinned, gutted, cut into small lumps and went into the cooking pot. That night we had a luxury meal, fresh horse meat stew. It was delightful and it put heart into us. We turned in with full bellies for once and with smiles on our faces.

The strange absence of German aircraft had not really registered on our minds. The first we were to see were just over the River Danube at Straubing. We had reached the bridge and been halted. The bridge had been mined ready for blowing up, but there did not appear to be anybody about to do the job. We could see the large aircraft bombs lashed to vital parts of the bridge with the wires already attached. We had to wait to get the all clear to cross.

Looking around us we saw on the other bank and not more than a couple of hundred yards from the bridge a hospital, clearly marked with a large red cross on the roof. At either end of the bridge the road had been torn up by massive craters, the bridge apparently untouched. The hospital, one might have thought, would be damaged by such a bombardment, but they would be wrong, it had not received a scratch, not a tile gone, not a window broken. The raid on the bridge had been pinpoint bombing.

Having finally received the all clear to cross the bridge, we started off once more. Once over the bridge, it was only a short distance to the main part of the town. At first we could see no signs of any damage. No buildings seemed to be touched and no bomb craters. Furthermore, no population that we could see.

Then following the main road round a corner we saw the first signs of damage. There were chips out of walls at first, then as we went further on we began to see heavier damage, holes in walls, roof damage and evidence of cannon fire and shrapnel damage. We were not prepared for what we saw when we reached the main town square.

Here, in the centre of town, the proof of accurate bombing became clear. There was, in effect, no town centre. All the main buildings were a mass of dust and rubble. The railway station had become a desolate heap of wreckage, the ruins of rolling stock showing through and atop the rubble, all burned out and still smouldering. So too were the buildings along the main street. A whole area had been wiped out. We understood that the raid that caused this havoc had taken place seven days before we arrived there.

It was outside Straubing, at the airfield, that we saw the reason for there being a lack of German fighter planes about. The main hangars could be seen quite plainly, well what was left of them, they had been neatly gutted, by either rocket or cannon fire. Around the field perimeter there were blast screens of earth in which planes were hidden, or the Germans thought they were hidden. Looking into these shelters as we passed, we could see wrecked and in many cases burnt out, planes, Me's and Fokkers. Out in the open all over the field were other planes in completely non-flying condition, having been worked over well by the Allied aircraft.

At another point a short distance from Straubing, we had not been long started on the days march, when we were halted in the shelter of some trees alongside the road. The reason was an air strike on a nearby airstrip. From our vantage point, we could see the Allied planes diving on the airstrip and then letting go their rockets. This was the first time I, and many others, had seen rockets fired from aircrafts. Soon, a thick black pall of smoke began to rise from the point of the attack.

Earlier at one of the overnight stops, before reaching Straubing, a nasty incident occurred. We still had a few Canadians with us and after rising on this particular day, one of the Canadians decided, after his morning ablutions, to see if he could walk off without being noticed. Unfortunately he was out of luck and when challenged by a sentry, promptly gave himself up. However, the evil minded Unteroffizier in charge of the section, ignoring all explanations, shot the man dead.

It was the end of the third week in April now and instead of moving off early in the morning as usual, we were told to stay put. The International Red Cross officials had paid a visit and informed us that an issue of parcels awaited us at our next stop. So we stayed where we were until the evening and then performed an over night march. We were taking our time, so I doubt the distance was very great.

Dawn saw us travelling downhill to an isolated farming hamlet nestling at the foot of the slope. We found out later that this hamlet was but a few miles from the town of Landshut, which also boasted an airfield.

Soon we were ensconced in large barns and once the parcels were issued, a brew quickly made and then sleep became the all important item. In a remarkably short time, the loudest noise to be heard were the resounding snores. However, sleep was to be interrupted by the arrival of some conscripts from a contingent of Hungarians. They did not want to fight for Germany, they just wanted to surrender to the American forces grouped not far away from us. They told us that there were several thousands of them and that the American 3rd Army was just across the valley and would we put in a good word for them when we were picked up by the Americans. We agreed to do their bidding and off they went back to the small wood they were hiding in. The Germans had made it clear that morning, that they intended to leave us to our fate, so we were not concerned one bit to give our word to the Hungarians.

But our dreams were to be shattered. At about 17.00 back came the Germans and told us to be ready to move off by 18.00. It was eventually 19.00 when we did finally move off. We cursed our luck and wondered how much longer would we be wandering around the German countryside before meeting Allied troops.

As it turned out, the Germans actually did us a good turn that night, for as we disconsolately marched back the way we had come, it was disheartening for us. Not far up the hill a cart track turned off to the right and we turned on to this. The rear end of the column had barely time to get safely on to the path when down rained a hail of shells. Below us and right up the road shells were exploding in, it seemed, a never ending hail of fire.

As we got further along the path we could see in the distance the flashes of the artillery from the American side and now the shells were whining over our heads at some unseen target over the hill top. The German 88's were giving some sort of an answer, there would be short sharp bursts of fire from the German side. So we had the sharp banging of the German 88's on one side and the whine of shells passing overhead in a non-stop howl from the other side.

With this barrage going on, something began to lift us and we burst forth into the good old war time songs, songs from both world wars. The Germans told us to shut up, but we only sang all the louder. Finally it was only shortage of breath through climbing along the path that stopped our singing. In the end, we passed round a shoulder of the hill and lost sight of the battle behind us.

The next morning found us well down in a deep valley, marching along a good road which ran alongside a river. Several small villages were passed through and all the time we could hear the tide of battle gradually passing round us. Then, later in the day, the sounds of battle died away.

It was the last week of April now, I think the 25th April 1945. From now on everything went much the same as before, although the weather had turned changeable and colder, with showers making life uncomfortable. By now we were a rag-tag bunch of men, dirty and lousy and rather ragged in dress. However, we did our best to look like the victors when passing through villages, for we could not let any German see that we were anything other than the winners.

1st May 1945. The weather turned bitterly cold and what had started as sleet now turned to a blinding snowstorm. We trudged along the road with our spirits at an all time low. When would this confounded march end? We kept asking ourselves. Somewhere around midday we arrived at a village name Buchbach and were stopped in the middle of the village, right where another road made a 'T' junction with the one we were on.

From out of the houses and shops close at hand came the members of the Deutschers Volksturm, the equivalent of our Home Guard, armed with a variety of weapons and took up strategic positions around us, while our guards disappeared to find quarters for the night presumably. The time ticked by and we got colder and colder, trying hard not to show our discomfort in front of these Bavarian peasants. After all, we were British and best.

We must have been standing there for almost an hour before the guards put in an appearance again. We marched off once more, with snow still falling, but now thinning. Later in the afternoon, the snow turned to light rain and then stopped. Much later, when it seemed that we had walked miles from the village, we were suddenly peeled off in our companies of 250 into four separate barns, these were to be our billets for the night.

Somewhere about 20.00 when most of us were thinking of turning in, somebody said that he thought he could hear tanks. As if to give his words credence, a very excited Frenchman rushed into the farmyard. Stuttering in his Gallic excitement, he managed to yell out that some American tanks were on the way. Scorn and derision were heaped upon him. He must be trying to pull our legs. He has seen or heard retreating German tanks. No, they were not, protested the Frenchman, he had seen the big white star on their sides. No, we said, that must have been a dirty great red star you saw, you only thought it was white.

Now, however, came a confirmation that we could not wave away as fantasy. A German farm worker came along and told us he had been standing outside his front door, when this tank came along wearing a big white star on its side. Then, he told us, the gun swung round and a shot was fired right through his front door. This seemed to verify the fact that American tanks were in the immediate vicinity.

Our Doctor and R.S.M. were informed and they persuaded the German Oberfeldwebel to accompany them with one of the guards up on to the road and, if more tanks appeared, they would stop one and find out just whose they were.

Not long after, three more tanks appeared and sure enough, they were American tanks. Having confirmed who we were, in next to no time at all, into the farmyard appeared one American Captain with three troopers. The German guards had surrendered and they were disarmed and locked away for the night.

We were told then, by the Americans, that Buchbach was only a matter of about a mile across the fields and if we wanted to, then one of his men would lead us into the village. We were not loathe to take advantage of this offer, so off we went following the soldier who drove a jeep, quite slowly I might say, into the village. He pointed out where we could find shelter, but also told us the village was ours and let no Germans deny us that. What we needed we could have - free. If there were any complaints, tell the military and they would soon deal with the offending Hun. (Krauts, the Yanks called them).

There still remained in our rough, ragged make-up, a sense of chivalry, being in captivity for so long had not dimmed our inborn sense of decency. The best place in the village was obviously the local school, quite a fair sized building, but which was occupied by three very frightened school mistresses, one of whom had an ailment which kept her bed bound. They must have felt very scared at the invasion of the school by a horde of ragged toughies, who were rough looking to say the least. However, the only thing we wanted to do in their quarters was to boil water on their stove so that we could have a brew.

For the rest, we bedded down in classrooms, stores, even in the loft. Our main thought that evening was sleep in a warm dry place. In the morning we would all go into the village and see what we could scrounge, beg, borrow or steal.

Ever since we had arrived at the village school it seemed that the Germans were intent on keeping us on our toes during the night, for every so often, we heard the sharp crack of a pair of 88's and the moan of the shells as they passed overhead. At one time, the calls of nature were so strong that I went down to the back entrance of the school with the intention of finding a toilet. Just as I was opening the door, quite a heavy wooden one, so a pair of shells landed a few feet away and dead in line with the door. I had that door closed quick as lightning, while the dirt and other debris smacked against the door. Calls of nature were instantly forgotten until some time later when we heard the sound of the firing fading into the distance.

The following morning I and my three constant consorts in crime, moved into the village and there set up our quarters in the local guesthouse. In Britain these would be called road houses, for they were only restaurants with overnight accommodation and not very good at that. While the two of us raided the spud locker, or store, and got our booty peeled and cooking, the other two went off foraging for something a bit more substantial, such as meat of some kind.

Remembering what we had been told, 'The village is yours, take what you want', they came back with four freshly killed chickens. Apparently the owner had not quite liked it and had quibbled over the poultry in not very kind words and had been told to shut his foul face or the Military would sort him out and he would land in clink, alongside our late guards.

It would appear that the Yanks had asked some of the lads if there were any of the guards who had not played the game and who needed sorting out. When told by the remaining Canadians what had happened they were told to help themselves to the captive guards and to their weaponry. Off went the Canadians, complete with German submachine guns and the offending Unteroffizier who had shot their chum in cold blood. They didn't have him with them when they returned. We also heard that the Hauptman (Captain) who had been in overall charge of the column had taken his staff car, driven into the woods and shot himself.

All through 2nd May, American troops were passing through the village. Infantry, armour, back-up motorised columns, all the full paraphernalia of war. One Private who dropped out for a rest and smoke, on seeing us said very plaintively, "We've been marching now for the least three weeks and haven't seen a goddammed sight of a single Kraut. Where are they?" Being wags we at once replied, "Over in the local nick, they are our ex-guards".

The passing American troops, on seeing us ragged lot, would stop and sling out cartons of cigarettes, usually by an officer riding in a jeep. These jeeps seemed to be full of the good things of life.

On 3rd May, about mid morning, a convoy of open trucks drove up. These had been sent to pick us now ex-P.o.W.'s up and transport us to a camp which, we were informed, was close by. About 60kms I heard somebody say. It was noticeable that all the truck drivers were negroes and the whole convoy led by a jeep, in the standard American practice.

Once loaded, off we went in close formation. These truck drivers were amazingly skilful in their handling of these large trucks, keeping the same tight and close formation at quite high speeds along some roads that had to be negotiated carefully because of battle damage. All around us we saw the litter of battle, shattered tanks, lorries, half tracks, guns and other burned out vehicles, all in twisted and battered heaps. The marks of the wheels and tracks stood out clearly in the soft earth, cris crossing each other like an unrolled ball of wool that had been thrown down.

Our destination turned out to be Stalag 7A, the first camp us ex-Italian P.o.W.'s had landed in when brought up to Germany. Now it was destined to be the last camp I, and many others, were to see. On arrival, we were lined up and then led to where a portable shower had been rigged up. Here we were given towel and soap and were allowed to indulge in the first shower we had been able to have over the past four months. The water may have been only luke warm, but as the grime of months of marching rolled off, I began to feel like a new man, it gave me a feeling of well being. That first shower was wonderful, the feeling it gave just cannot be adequately described.

Having redressed ourselves we were lined up again. The Stalag was already full to overflowing with all the columns converging on it, so we were to be sent to an outlying farm. This farm was only a short distance from the Stalag, less than a mile. Before we were allowed to enter the farm precincts we had to be deloused, so we had to line up in a field just outside the farm.

Watching the proceedings was a audience of small boys and a few girls. Watching the Medical Orderlies stuffing the DDT gun up our trouser legs, down the tops of our trousers, up the arms of our jackets and in fact anywhere and everywhere they could and the stray puffs of powder which blew up into our noses causing us to sneeze, had become a source of innocent merriment to these youngsters.

The powder was very effective though and after the application and a minute or two had passed, it seemed that all the lice in the universe were doing a war dance cum rock and roll all over the body. Perhaps another minute or two and everything quietened down to normal, but without the itching.

The audience of small boys and not so small girls were soon put to flight by the simple expedient of giving them a puff of powder up their kilts. They didn't like that.

The delousing completed, we were lined up again and given some strict instructions. We were to treat the farmer as we would treat one of our own farmers, not to interfere in any way with the running of the farm, treat the farm property with the same respect you would your own, no stealing of farm stock, nor any foraging for food. Any felony would be dealt with as a Military Offence. Also fresh food would be sent up each day in sufficient quantity to satisfy our needs. Now we could proceed into the farm and find our billets.

Our billets were much the same as on the march, except that we were now in clean outhouses. My kitbag cum rucksack now contained my last remaining possessions, apart from what I stood up in, namely three electrical text books which had been sent me while a prisoner, I still have these books each with the Italian Censors stamp on two of them and the German Censors stamp on the third. My lasting memories of being a Prisoner of War.

CHAPTER ELEVEN

Returning Home

The Americans were better than their word about the food. In our minds they did us proud. Unused to such things as we were now, the first thing to open our eyes wide was the issue of pure white bread. We had forgotten what it looked like. To our wondering eyes it took the appearance of snowy white puffs of cotton wool, only this cotton wool happened to be eatable. It takes imagination to gauge our feelings at the first bite and taste of that white succulent soft bread. How reverently we handled it. So long had we been used to firstly the wholemeal bread in Britain, then the straw coloured bread of Italy, absolutely tasteless, the almost black bread of Germany and quite recently the sour tasting potato bread issued to the German Army, bread which had probably been wrapped and stock-piled for years before it saw the light of day.

The rest of the daily rations consisted in the main of the American 'K' ration packs, issued in threes, breakfast, dinner and supper. Each pack contained toilet paper, cigarettes, matches in one of them and tinned foods which although not looking very much, contained all the proteins, vitamins, starch etc, that we need to remain fit(?) and healthy. Of course, the cigarettes were a most welcome item.

After our arrival, we had each been given a telegraph form to fill in, if we so required, to let our families know we were safe and sound. I filled mine in and told myself "That's okay. You've let them know you are safe and well and will soon be home." As I was to remark later, so much for telegrams sent from the Continent.

There was little to do except wander round the farm, we had been warned to stay close in case we got a hurry up and leave call. So it was mainly remain in the confines of the farm, or doze in the sun, as the weather had now turned warm and bright.

On 8th May everybody in billets on the farm got the prepare to leave immediately message. We were ready in no time. By mid-morning an impressive fleet of trucks had arrived at the farm. The huge convoy soon filled up with hopeful ex-P.o.W.'s and with hearts uplifted were soon on our way. Destination - Landshut airfield.

On arrival at the airfield, we disembarked and were told to arrange ourselves into groups of 28. This was the highest number the aircraft could safely take. Having sorted ourselves out and been put under the charge of an N.C.O. there was nothing more to do but wait patiently. Looking round, there seemed to be thousands already waiting there, so our chances of getting away seemed very slim.

Under the circumstances and as could be expected, there were the usual prangs, to use R.A.F. parlance, with planes being taken out of service for repairs, thus making the wait longer. Then a shower softened the ground and some planes tended to get stuck in patches of mud and finish up on their noses. We must remember that these old planes were DC3's, the Dakota's. Wonderful planes, but dead slow. All these accidents brought gloom upon us, our hearts sank.

Flying ceased at dusk. We then had to find our way back into town to find a place to bed down for the night. After careful and considered thought, our gang of four decided on a spare room in a block of flats. I grant you that this room was in the attic, but it was dry and free from draughts and it had a garret window through which we could look out over the town and admire the dismal view of shattered buildings and flattened houses.

Two of us did venture out to see if there was another, perhaps better, billet but after investigating one empty building, the side walls of which were boarded up, the entrance hall a mass of rubble and although the building had, as we found, a bedroom complete with double bed and torn curtains over glassless windows, there was a smell of death over the whole place. The two of us decided that the flat was by far the best spot, even lacking the comfort of a bed.

Quite apart from that, it was highly dangerous to venture too far at night. The Americans had imposed a curfew on the German populace from dusk until dawn. As we well knew, the Yanks were a trigger happy lot and shot at anything that moved if it looked the slightest bit suspicious. What would we have appeared in our ragged state? Highly suspicious I would have thought. As it so happened, during the night, we did hear the sound of shots being fired.

Some time after full dark had fallen, although there was moonlight, we heard the sound of German aero engines. Suddenly it seemed that the whole anti-aircraft defences opened fire and for several minutes the air became full of flying tracer reaching skyward and H.E.

bursting high above our perch. Just as suddenly it all stopped and we sat wondering what it had all been about.

Foraging around the flat and some of the other areas of the block, between us we found a half full bottle of wine, potatoes and pickled eggs. This set us up for a reasonably good meal before we turned in. A supper of fried eggs and spuds, just what we had waited for and just what the doctor ordered.

The next morning, 9th May, we were up and about bright and early. We had to get back to the airfield pretty smartly as flying commenced at 08.00. On arriving there we settled into our groups of 28 and settled down to await our turn to board one of the many planes available.

Now we could see what all the commotion of the previous night had been all about, for lined up at one end of the field were an assortment of German planes. These had all come in to surrender, hence the trigger happy firing of the A.A. defences the previous night. What an assortment, Me.110's, Fw.190's, Heinkels, Dorniers and others. I did not think the Germans had that many aircraft left after what we had seen during the march.

To cap it all it began to rain. Not a light drizzle, but a heavy rain and the airfield being only a grass one, the runway soon became a mud patch. Soon planes standing on the runway began to sink into the mud and, to add to our growing worries, two or three came to grief trying to land.

Word immediately came round to regroup in groups of 24, that being the most the planes could carry and take off with under the present conditions. At least, that was the official reason and they should know best.

Gloom, even deeper than before greeted this arrangement. Soon, however the rain stopped and the ground slowly began to dry under a warm sun and a light breeze. By mid-afternoon the runway was hard enough for the planes to start carrying their original loads of 28, so we regrouped once more into groups of 28, making us all much happier.

Whilst waiting, the old proverbial 'K' rations were issued by an American soldier, who brought round the requisite number for each group at the right time. There were so many ex-P.o.W.'s that the ration packs could not be issued indiscriminately in case there should be a shortage.

Over on the far side of the airfield stood a barn. In that barn a number of British P.o.W.'s had been put. To save themselves from being hit during the air raids, they had managed to find some white paint and brushes and had crawled out on to the roof and painted P.O.W.'s in huge letters which filled the roof either side from ridge to gutter.

The second day ended as had the first, with no sign of getting away and still with huge numbers waiting to go before us. Back to the town we went and back into our former lodgings.

This time, whilst two of us were wandering about, I and the one with me opened a door and found ourselves face to face with a young German and, I presume, his wife. Although the girl looked frightened, the young man beckoned us to enter. We spoke for a few minutes and indicated that we would like to do a bit of cooking, if the couple didn't mind. We got the affirmative and that became another hurdle cleared. I remember the relief on the girl's face that showed when she realised we meant no harm to her or her man.

10th May was a repeat of the previous two days, at least until late evening. Then at about 19.00, three aircraft came in and it was announced that these were the last three flying for that day. Our group was one of the lucky ones, we got the very last plane.

At 19.30 we were airborne and waving goodbye to Landshut and saying a very relieved goodbye to Germany. We flew at 3,000 feet and before full darkness set in, the terrain below could be read as if it were a book. All the horrors of total war lay exposed to the eye, the ravished, torn and battered countryside had no way of hiding its scars from our all seeing eyes above,

About 22.30 the plane touched down at Reims. I say touched down, for that is just what the plane did and bounced all along the runway until it stopped. This runway was one of those metal strip runways that were developed during the war. From the way that plane careered along that runway, I had ghastly visions for a moment, of us coming to a grinding halt in the middle of some ruined airport buildings that could just be seen ahead.

On leaving the plane, we were taken to a large building in which there were literally thousands of Service personnel going about their business. Apparently this was a transit camp of some sort, where one could get a hot meal and a bed for the night before proceeding to wherever one may be going.

We were shown where to sleep and where to get a meal and warned to be up early in the morning, as the first 1,000 ready and waiting outside would be the first to get home.

That was enough incitement for me and my three fellow criminals. It was eat, sleep and the first one up shake the others. We didn't sleep much, for we were awake and had eaten and were on the road outside by 06.00 the following morning. There lined up on the opposite side of the road stood a fleet of lorries, the drivers standing by their vehicles.

Along came an officer and he soon had us lined up and sorted out into groups of 24, giving each block a number. That was the number of the lorry we were to board and also the number of the plane we were to board at the R.A.F. airfield the other side of Reims.

Having boarded the lorries, they then moved off and once clear of the airfield drove as if all the demons in hell were after them. Passing through the streets of Reims, people waved at us and cheered, many of them having to do a quick hop to one side to avoid being run down, there being little room for avoiding action by the lorry drivers. On reaching the airfield, the lorries drove round the perimeter track, then along a runway to where what seemed to be a whole squadron of bombers stood waiting. The lorries then stopped in front of the aircraft that had been assigned to them.

This lot were a squadron of Lancaster bombers and this was the first time I had made an acquaintance with them. At close quarters they were very impressive and far more business like than the old Dakota of the previous day.

We disembarked from the lorries and were met by the air crews who had been standing by their aircraft awaiting our arrival. We were soon in conversation with the crew members, a friendly lot who made us feel at home. They were all interested in who we were and where we had come from and all the other details we could give in answer to their questions.

Before embarking in the plane, we had a last cigarette, were issued with a box of sweets and a grease-proof bag, the bag being, as one of the crew put it, to puke in if you feel airsick. As he remarked, it was amazing the number of chaps who were sick once they got into the air.

Our meagre baggage was stowed in the bomb bay and we embarked on the plane. As the plane was still fully armed and ready for instant action, we had to spread out along the length of the aircraft and keep clear of the crew going about their jobs. Maybe we were a bit cramped, but we were on our way home and in a British aircraft and in about three hours time would be stepping out on to the soil of good old England once more.

Everything in this Lancaster was so smooth that I never even felt the aircraft take off and it came as a bit of a surprise when one of the crew came along and told us we could move around a bit if we liked and invited us to take a peep through the mid upper gunners position.

The whole flight of some 30 or more planes flew at 5,000 feet and soon the navigator came along to tell us that we were over the Channel. Down below one of my comrades told me there were three destroyers steaming at high speed, but before I could get a look they were past and gone.

Brighton slid by below and shortly we were coming in to land. Our landing was at an airfield near Winchester, I believe it was Worthy Down. So gentle was the landing, that I was surprised to see the exit door opening and one of the air crew making his way out of the plane.

On stepping from the plane, I was startled to see what appeared to be a full meeting of the Combined Staff. There were Naval officers of varying ranks from Captain down to 'Snotties' (Midshipmen), all mingled with Army and R.A.F. 'Brass Hats' and others.

Now, as I was not wearing my greatcoat, the Royal Navy flashes I had made in Italy and sewn on stood out on my battle dress jacket. In a flash, the Senior Naval Officer spotted my flashes. With a hearty roar of greeting he stepped forward, hand outstretched. I hardly remember what he said, but I know he was giving me a really warm and heartfelt welcome home. Once he had finished shaking my hand the process was repeated by all the other Naval officers and the Army and R.A.F. officers.

In the meantime it had been 'Bombs away' with our odd bits of luggage. It had been dropped from the bomb bay of the aircraft. Now, as we picked up our bits and pieces, we were warned that if we wished to get something to eat we had best be catching that wagon that was just about to push off. There was a hurried scramble to get on and with bodies hanging on by their eyebrows, off it shot, grossly overloaded, toward the reception centre.

Arriving at the reception centre, a long row of tables set up beside a large tent, I dumped my small piece of luggage and made my way up to one of the tables. Here I was given another of those forms for Allied P.o.W.'s Recovered to fill in. On this I had to enter as much detail as possible, name, rank, number, date of capture, date of recovery and by whom.

Completing the form, I was then directed into the tent. This proved to be another delousing centre and I was subjected to the same process I had been through when first retaken by the Americans. After delousing, I wandered out of the tent and went to pick up my kit.

I was in for yet another surprise. Just as I had found my gear and as yet uncertain where to go, a W.A.A.F. came up. She went to take my gear from me, but I would not let her do so. However, she insisted, so I let her take my greatcoat, the only decent piece of clothing I now possessed.

In next to no time she put me at my ease. I had often wondered how it would be and how I would react when I first met up with a member of the opposite sex, but somehow her manner, charm and the way she acted quite natural, as if I had never been away from home for such a long time, made me feel easy and I found myself talking as if I had known her all my life.

The waiting room, if you could call it that, was the cinema. On entering I received a packet of ten cigarettes and a booklet of matches and from a Red Cross woman a linen bag which contained shaving gear and a block of chocolate. Once inside, my W.A.A.F. guide took me to a table, got tea and biscuits. I was not feeling hungry now and we sat talking for some time before she had to leave, presumably to help with another crowd of returning prisoners I expect.

The came the announcement. All Naval personnel to report at the desk under the stage. Here I had to give name, number, rating and ship and was told to hold myself in readiness to leave when piped for.

Shortly after this the pipe came for all Naval personnel to muster outside at a certain point. Out I went and met up with a few more matelots.

It was while waiting here that three more W.A.A.F.'s came along. Seeing who we were, they sat down on the grass with us and talked and joked with us. After a while, they got their heads together and one of them went off, returning after a short while with several packets of cigarettes. These they gave to us and they would not be refused and to this day I am certain that those three girls spent their last few pennies to provide the cigarettes and left themselves short of both cash and cigarettes for the rest of the week.

The Naval bus eventually turned up and we piled aboard. There was a hearty waving of hands and cheerful shouted goodbyes as the bus pulled away. The driver told us we were bound for Stockheath, near Havant.

The bus arrived at Stockheath Naval Camp about 14.30. This memorable day of becoming a member of the Royal Navy again was Friday 11th May 1945. After we had disgorged from the bus, there was the minor matter of an interrogation to go through, this being conducted by a Chief Wren.

This interrogation took the form of asking such things as, did you attempt escape, or escape attempts made by groups. Had you been made to work in Germany? Did you perform any acts which might be classed as sabotage? (Yes). These sort of questions plus the normal name, rating, number, ship, date of capture, where captured, by whom captured, when retaken, what date, where and by whom? After this we could, if we wished, send a telegram free of charge to our families to inform them we were safe and sound.

Having the other telegram in mind, I chose not to send one from here. I received a voucher with which I could get a made to measure uniform should I so choose and set off for the dining hall.

My first cooked meal in England after three years. An enormous plate of eggs and chips was placed in front of me and a large mug of strong tea. I ate as much as I could, but I am afraid the size of the meal beat me, I was full before I was half way through it.

Next on the list was the M.O. who asked if I had anything wrong with me. I, of course, being perfectly honest, well almost perfectly honest, replied that I was as fit as a fiddle (almost) and he muttered something to the effect of "Only time will tell that" and passed me fit.

Next stop the Dentist. He took a quick look at my molars and others, gave a grunt and passed me fit. From the Dentist the next stop was the Pussers Clothing Store, where I was issued with a survivors kit, which means just the bare essentials, one uniform, blue. Two sets underwear, white. Two white fronts. One jersey, blue. Two collars, one black silk, one pair shoes, black. Two pairs socks, blue. One towel, cap, cap tally. Just enough to keep me going until I received a full kit on reaching my own Depot, Chatham.

The dormitories here were Nissen huts. I believe that Stockheath had previously been an R.A.F. camp and had been taken over by the Royal Navy. As it always is with a sailor the World over, when he has to live in a place, he makes it a home from home. This was no exception. The hut was spotless, warm and the inmates very cheerful, contented and friendly. In the flash of an eye, a mug of tea was placed in my hand and I was given a toast for a happy return and a good leave.

There remained one thing, a thorough bath and to get out of the filthy gear I was wearing. The bath house was just across from the hut and once there, I revelled in the glorious feeling of steaming hot water pouring over my tired body. I do not know how long I stayed under that shower, turning and letting the hot water play over me, soaping myself again and again. On emerging from the shower and drying, the feel of fresh clean clothes was perfect heaven to me.

Once in bed, sleep came easily. For over a year now I had slept on hard boards and in barns and straw. The feel of a, what was to me, soft bed, lulled me off to sleep in no time.

12th May 1945. In the morning I was awakened by one of the hut inmates, who held a mug of tea for me. After drinking that, I was soon up and washed and dressed. Breakfast over and my new bit of kit packed, I made my way to the Regulating Office, where I received my leave pass, railway warrants and ration cards, with a set of instructions as to what I should do. I received some pay, with the warning that the rest would be sent on to me from my own Depot.

The glorious moment came when the buses came to take all us going on leave to Havant Station. The poor old porteress at the barrier was left in a state of confusion. For days now, large numbers of sailors had been passing through that barrier, mostly ex-P.o.W.'s now she didn't know one from the other.

As the dear old porteress said, New entries and ex-P.o.W.'s all looked alike in brand new suits, ready made of course from the Pussers Store and wearing Pussers crabs (boots or shoes from Naval issue). I must admit, I looked just like a New Entry myself with my issued kit and trimmings. I felt like one too, just like I felt with my first uniform as a boy at H.M.S. "GANGES".

The London (Waterloo) train was fairly crowded, but I managed to get a corner seat and tried to shrink down into it and look as if I were not there. I really felt uncomfortable, the civilians in the compartment kept looking at me as if they could not quite make up their minds definitely who or what I was.

At Waterloo, I hurriedly crossed to the Eastern Section, found the platform from which my local train would depart and impatiently waited the few minutes for which the train took to travel from Charing Cross. On arrival, I tried to find an empty compartment, but my luck was out. However, this being a local train, the occupants of the compartment I got in seemed blissfully ignorant of the fact that I was there. Too many Service men about in London I presumed. I still felt awkward and embarrassed and hoped that when I reached my station, I could walk the short distance without being spotted by somebody I knew.

My luck was in this time. I had taken my time reaching the barrier when I got off the train and left the station at the end of a small crowd who had also reached their destination. Looking all round me, I set off down the alley that led to the road along which I had to travel. All the rest of the way home I was peering at anybody I saw, ready to do a vanishing act if I recognised them. I did not wish to speak to anybody about anything before I reached the safety of my own home.

How glad I was when I reached my front gate without being seen by anybody I knew. There lay a welcome home that one only dreams about. It was a hot day and the front door lay wide open. I slowly and quietly walked to the wide open front door and entered. My Father was sitting in his usual place at meal times, I could just see the back of his head and a side view of the rest of his body, but no sign of anybody else, but I could hear voices. Saturday lunch was in the course of being consumed. Trust me to arrive just as this time.

I had put down my steaming bag and turned toward the kitchen door when something gave me away, some slight noise I had made perhaps and my Father turned and saw me. I well remember his words, "It's Mac!"

Then he was out of his chair and shaking my hand, my Mother had her arms wrapped round me and was kissing me, while dancing round the pair of them was my sister, crying her eyes out and trying to get into the melee. Of my young brother, there was no sign, but I gathered when all the fuss and hubbub had died down, that he was out earning a bob or two helping one of the milkmen.

When little brother did finally arrive, he stood behind me grinning like an ape and then when I did set eyes on him, I nearly asked who he was, he had altered so much as he grew up. I only remembered him in short trousers, a scruffy little schoolboy. As he had been evacuated at the outbreak of war, I had only seen him once in May 1940, that time was after the Narvik affair. Five years does make a lot of difference, but, unfortunately, I was still his hero big brother (although I shall never know why).

That evening, I had another very pleasant surprise. A very old friend from the "GANGES"/"RAMILLIES"/"RESOLUTION" days who had transferred to the Fleet Air Arm put in an appearance. Roy and I had been very close friends and now there he was, resplendent in his Sub-Lt.'s uniform, standing on the doorstep. His first remark was "I had a feeling you would be home today". He too, was on leave, so I just had to go with him to pay my respects to his parents and his wife and son and have a good natter about the missing years.